Cuckoo Town

Dales Life in the 1950s

Cuckoo Town
Dales Life in the 1950s

by

W R Mitchell

Illustrations
by
IONICUS

CASTLEBERG
2000

For
MARGARET
A Daleswoman at Heart

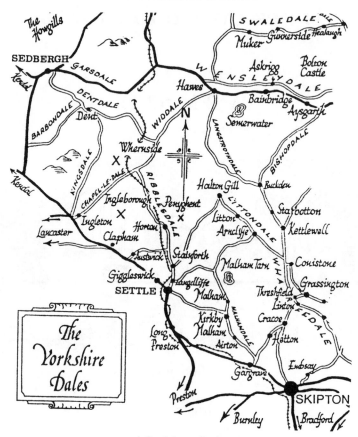

A **Castleberg** Book.
First published in the United Kingdom in 2000.
Text, © W R Mitchell 2000.
The moral right of the author has been asserted.
ISBN 1 871064 59 7
Typeset in New Baskerville, printed and bound in the United Kingdom by
Lamberts Print & Design, Station Road, Settle, North Yorkshire, BD24 9AA.
Published by Castleberg, 18 Yealand Avenue, Giggleswick, Settle, North
Yorkshire, BD24 0AY.

Contents

Illustrations

Front cover painting by Percy Monkman

The illustrations by IONICUS (Jos Armitage) are used by courtesy of his daughter, Lesley Shepherd

Drawing of Austwick in the Thirties by Godfrey Wilson

The picture of a curlew on page 75 was drawn by Richard Bancroft

Austwick in the Thirties

Prologue

Cuckoo *(Cuculus canorus) n. Migratory bird of the family Cucculidae with characteristic note or cry. Winters in Africa and reaches British Isles in April, depositing its eggs in nests of small birds.*

Cuckoo *(Cuculus austwicki) n. Migratory bird with an aversion to walls being built round its roost. Last seen in days of yore.*

Cuckoo Town was a name given to Austwick, a straggling village typical of many in the Yorkshire dale-country. Here is a light-hearted account of people and happenings at Austwick in the halcyon days of the mid-20th century when every other person was a character and there was a strong sense of community. My family and I lived in the village for seven years. It was a frugal life, but there was joy in little things.

Austwick was noted for its daft tales. The folk we knew in the 1950s were not averse to telling them. The best known story related to a time when cuckoos called all day in spring and early summer. Some of the villagers, mindful that the cuckoo brought good weather, and that conditions deteriorated when it had departed to its winter quarters, saw a bird roosting in a tree. They discussed the matter, then spent the night building a wall around the tree. At first light, the cuckoo flew over the wall. The wallers, though disappointed, were convinced that if they had put another row or two of stones on the wall all would have been well.

Austwick had its "whittle tree". It was one of two immense trees standing near the church. A whittle, you should know, is a small knife that was favoured by butchers. When this was the only knife in the village, it was suspended from a branch of t'whittle tree until someone required it. If there was no whittle, he or she would tour the village shouting: "Whittle to t'tree."

The whittle was lost when workmen, having taken it to Swarthmoor, and needing it on the following day, decided to stick it in the ground. In the absence of trees, it was left at the edge of a cloud shadow. Next day, the whittle could not be found. The cloud had moved.

The name Austwick relates to its position "east of Clapham." No love was lost between the two villages. They were as chalk and cheese. Austwick men were known as carles and they gave the Clapham men the disrespectful name of clouts. Perhaps the "cuckoo tales" were promoted by Clapham as a form of revenge.

The stories were truly daft. It was said that an Austwick man who came across a watch in a lane heard it ticking and thought it was a venomous reptile. Neighbours were called. The bravest of them killed the "reptile" with a pick-axe. An Austwick farmer tried to lift a bull out of one of his fields. Nine friends helped him. After five hours of struggle, one of them hit on the idea of opening the gate.

A local saying was to the effect that "the best's at the bottom." A man who fell into a pond and was drowning made gurgling noises that were interpreted by his friends as "good, good, good." No one went to help him. A calf fattened in an upper room at a house grew so big the window had to be removed when it was decided to move it. When some of the houses were thatched, a farmer noticed the grass was sprouting on one of them. He hoisted up two or three cows to pasture it off.

Even dafter was the tale of an Austwick farmer who wheeled an empty barrow in and out of a barn. He said he was taking in sunshine to the hay, which had been damp when harvested. It was possibly the same man who took a wheelbarrow to Clapham railway station. Finding field paths offered a short cut, he cheerfully went by way of the fields – and had to lift the barrow over eleven stiles.

Nature was kind to Austwick. The village has a backdrop of limestone hills – Norber (the north hill), Moughton (nibbled at by quarrymen) and well-wooded Oxenber (where, 'tis said, oxen were kept when they were not pulling carts or ploughs). Austwick Beck has a wayward course over the Silurian rocks of Crummack Dale, flowing under several clapper-bridges. The old-time glacier deposited a scattering of dark-grey boulders on the flanks of Norber and when limestone around the huge stones was eroded they were left on pedestals of limestone, to be worshipped by geologists.

Tucked away in folds of the land are Austwick's satellite hamlets, if the proud residents do not mind me referring to them as such. The names are Feizor, Wharfe and, on the gritstone side of the fault-line, the scattered farms of Lawkland and Eldroth. The splendid Lawkland Hall was for many years the home of the Ingilbys who – says I, name-dropping – were related to the Ingilbys of Ripley Castle.

There was nothing darker than Feizor on a cloudy night, for then t'village lantern [the moon] had gone out. They had some daft ideas at Feizor, the daftest being that of the highest cottage where slabs sticking out from the chimney were said to be seats for tired witches, who hopefully would not molest the householder and his family. One of the Feizor houses was in two parishes. A dying man who was in a room belonging to Lawkland parish asked to be buried in Giggleswick, so he was moved into the next room (and parish). There was a saving on burial fees.

Wharfe has its back to Moughton and gives its name to a gill – an enormous V-shaped valley carved out by what is now the Ribble, which eventually found a new course. So "they" say, but as an old friend remarked: "They'll say owt." Eldroth Church (for years used as a school) is a modest house of prayer, built when local people who attended Austwick Church were frequently impeded by floods. Eldroth Hall is out of sight. The public hall was said to have been bought from contractors who built Harden Bridge isolation hospital. At dances, I entertained the thought that during the Palais Glide the building was likely to shift on its foundations. A new hall is in prospect.

Austwick could be as quiet as Aberdeen on a flag-day or so noisy they heard us in Clapham, a mile or two away. I've walked from one end of Austwick to the other in daylight and not seen a soul. At other times, I couldn't stir for folk. Any notable national event brought out the daftness and the desire to let off steam. There would be a torchlight procession. The best position was at the end. The others were likely to have candle-fat dribbled down their backs. Forty-five years ago, when we made our home at Austwick, the post office was presided over by Harry Lord, and his distinctive contribution was leaping over a bonfire made of almost-spent torches.

They were a canny lot in Austwick. A lady shopkeeper, on taking delivery of matches, removed one match from each box, which provided her with a free supply. Mrs Brewin, who was classifiable as an Angel, but had not yet been awarded her wings, provided an old reprobate, Dave Jack, with his Sunday dinner (on a silver tray). Her trim little figure might be seen carrying the laden tray across the village. If Dave Jack was grateful for her generosity, he never showed it. As Mrs Brewin entered his little cottage, he would be sitting at the fireside, with his back to the door. He did not even look round as he remarked, week by week, year in, year out: "Put it ower theer!"

Summer's pleasures included the Flower Show, known locally as the Lord's Day because the Lord family scooped most of the prizes. Autumn saw the start of the dancing season in the parish hall, with music provided by concertina and drums. The aforementioned Old Will, noticing that we were sitting out during one dance, commanded us to "git up – an' shak thi supper down!"

As the year waned, salmon nosed their way up Lune and Wenning to enter Austwick Beck. Watchers on the bridge saw lordly fish cruising like so many mini-submarines. Meanwhile, the farmers and their men had an unceasing round of milking and mucking-out. The landscape was dotted with outbarns, each of which held a few young bee-asts [cattle] and the hay, garnered from meadows round about, to sustain them through the long winter. A farmer who had five barns employed a young man to attend to them. This he did, twice a day. When someone sympathised with him, he replied: "I've always preferred walking to working." At times, he ran – and kept wondrously fit. Another farmer who had umpteen outbarns provided his perspiring farm man with one shovel and one brush, which were used for "mucking out." They had to be carried from one barn to another.

Winter walks were graded in length according to how we felt. Most of the villagers, including ourselves, did not have a car. The compensation was provided by the orange buses of the Pennine company, then operating an hourly service, with a late night bus on Saturday enabling us to enjoy the Ingleton fleshpots [cinema, known widely as the flea-pit, followed by patronage of the fish-and-chip shop]. A frail old lady who boarded the Pennine bus early in the afternoon booked for Skipton. She told the driver: "I'm bahn [going] to the hospital, lad. Drive carefully." He did. As she left the bus, she said: "Thank you. I made a jelly and when I set off for the bus it hadn't quite set."

Cuckoo Town never seemed the same after Queen Elizabeth II was crowned in. I'm not blaming Her Majesty, of course. It's just that one or two folk bought new-fangled television sets and invited their neighbours and friends to watch the proceedings at Westminster Abbey. We gawped at flickering black-and-white images on a nine-inch screen and declared them "wonderful."

Little did we know that the goggle-box would change not only our daily routine but our way of thinking. Or that on that day the cuckoo, neglected by the Austwickians, would quit the village for ever...

11

1 – First Impressions

From the windows of the train, I watched the landscape change from brown to white – from the gritstone of my native Skipton to the limestone of my adopted Austwick. The train was steam-hauled. Now and again, a curl of smoke obscured the view. I listened to the comforting *deh, deh, deh, dah* as the train beat a tattoo on the jointed rails.

For a milltown lad who had entered journalism by way of the local newspaper and had just spent two years of national service in the Navy – without actually going to sea – this train journey in 1948 would lead to a job with *The Dalesman* magazine and, in due course, to seven whimsical years in Cuckoo Town.

Above the seats in the compartment were framed photographs – sepia prints recalling the glories of a lost England: of Edwardian resorts and splendid landscapes. The train smoke cleared long enough for me to see a grey-green landscape, fields dotted with sheep, a bird-busy sky – and the domed chapel of Giggleswick School, perched on a gritstone knoll and looking for all the world like a jelly mould. As a small boy, being taken on holiday to Morecambe, I was told by a know-it-all in the carriage that the domed structure was an observatory. I felt cheated when I could not see a protruding telescope.

My gaze shifted to my fellow passenger who, to judge by his manner and clothes, was a farmer in his best setting-off suit. He also had a best setting-off crook – a stick of hazel topped by a tup's horn. A pipe-smoker, he was emitting almost as much smoke as the locomotive. The tweedy suit had doubtless been bought from Renshaws or Moores of Settle or at Breares, in Skipton High Street. You paid extra for quality. Many a farmer who purchased a suit for his wedding was still trying to wear it out forty years later.

My companion was small, thin and with a face as wizened as an unsteeped prune. He was, as they say in the Dales, "nobbut t'size o' twopennorth o' copper." He had the usual Dales farmer's accessory, this being the aforementioned tobacco pipe. It was a briar. In the Dales of the 1950s there were still men who drew the fumes from black twist up the thin but brittle stem of a clay pipe.

When he was not looking at me, I was looking at him. The eyes set under arches of grizzle-grey brows were bright – the sort you see on a fell-going sheep, though not at agricultural shows, where they always look dopey. Tufts of grey hair extended below the neb of his cap. The farmer, having pondered for a while, asked: "Whear's ta bahn?" (Where are you going?). I "telled" him.

There was a wheezy sound, like that of a gate swinging on rusty hinges. Was this little chap about to have a stroke? Then I realised he was laughing. He chided me with the words: "Tha means Cuckoo Town." More wheezing. "That's where they tried to keep summer by walling-in a cuckoo."

He transferred some more tobacco from pouch to pipe, pressed it down with what must have been an asbestos finger, and after creating a through draught with a noisy sucking sound, applied a match. In the still air of the compartment, the smoke took a while to clear.

"It's a queer shop, is Austwick," said he, inflicting a mortal wound on standard English. My travelling companion told a tale of the farm man who walked over Buckhaw Brow to Settle, having an appointment with the doctor. It was raining as he left the surgery. The doctor provided him with an umbrella. The man carried this wonderful contraption proudly back to his home, marvelling at the way the cloth canopy pro-tected him from a steady downpour.

Back home, the umbrella was too large to be taken into the house so it was tied up in a spare stall in the shippon. On the following market day, the farm man returned to Settle, holding the umbrella over his head. This time, he attracted attention. There wasn't a rain-cloud in the sky.

The train's *deh, deh, deh, dah* became a rumbling sound. "We're on t'viaduct, lad. Tha'd better look sharp." We disembarked on the long, draughty "down" platform at Clapham and crossed a footbridge so high it looked as though it might have a resident cloud.

Spring was bustin' out all over – to quote a popular song. Away to the west were the "vacant, wine-red moors" as described so vividly by Stevenson. A breeze carried to us a moorland tang. Or could it have been the muck from the outbarns, being spread using horse, cart and hand-fork? A curlew, big, streaky-brown, with down-curved mandibles, hung in the air like a feathered kite, then glided, uttering a bubbling trill as it surveyed its territory on stiffened wings. A starling, glossy in its spring finery, incorporated part of the curlew song in its reedy refrain from its chimney-top perch at the station. Sparrows chirped. Song thrushes were busy constructing a nest on a railway wagon in a rusty siding.

The stationmaster, resplendent in a well-creased uniform and a cap with "scrambled egg" on the neb, took a few tickets, slammed a few carriage doors and, addressing the farmer, gave the Dales head-jerk, a sign of recognition. He said: "Na then." What more could be said?

Clapham was a railway junction then. The main line took farmers to the auction at Bentham and eager holidaymakers to Lancaster and Morecambe. Dora and Ben Hudson once went on holiday to Morecambe. Dora told a friend: "He won't be there more than five minutes afore he's asking the way to Lancaster auction mart."

In the days I recall, a branch line extended from Clapham to Ingleton, where a big viaduct was strung across the valley like a Victorian cobweb. The line continued to Lunesdale, where it joined up with the Lancaster-Carlisle just south of Shap.

To the farm folk of Keasden, their farms spread alongside the road leading from Clapham station to Bowland, the railway was a vital link with the outer world for goods and services. It was known for a Keasden farmer to buy a tup at Kirkby Stephen and transport it home by train to Settle. He'd then tug it across the valley to entrain at Giggleswick station. By the time Clapham station was reached, the day would be far spent, as the Good Book says. Then "me and t'tup had to climb yon hill road. When we git home, we were both ready for summat to eat and a good sleep."

The farmer and I stood on the footbridge while he recovered the breath expended as he climbed a long flight of steps. He gave yet another wheezy laugh. "By gum, lad, but I feels nostalgic today. When you get to my age, there's nowt much else to do but rummage about among your memories."

He promptly told me about the coal-merchant who had his yard by the station. He was so precise when weighing out coal that he kept a dozen assorted cobs and used them on the scale until the customer had precisely the weight he had requested.

Beyond the station yard was a hotel called *The Flying Horseshoe*, featuring the aforementioned winged horseshoe. My farmer friend was bound for Clapham village, one and a-half miles away. His "lad" was due to pick him up, which he did. The "lad," a strapping six-footer, appeared in a car on which the dirt was so thick I harboured the notion that if he did not want to wash it, he might consider covering t'muck with pebble-dash.

Inside the car, it was breath-taking – literally. To collect his dad, the son had broken off work in this merry month of muck-spreading. To breathe in deeply was to have a sensation akin to having a rough file thrust down the throat. The ancient car bearing me to Clapham on that Spring day of long ago had an engine that rasped like that of a lovelorn corncrake.

The one and a-half mile link road had an aversion to going straight. We stopped for no reason at all, I thought, until I heard the thunder of hooves and a drove of lively horses passed. I was to get to know those horses well. They were supposed to live on the unfenced Newby Moor but had the freedom of the parish. A black horse perished on a dark night when it was hit by the bus.

I saw a skyline crowned by proud Ingleborough, one of the big Pennine flat-tops. "It's a chilly spot, even in summer. And it's got a lazy wind. It tries to go through thee rather than taking t'trouble to go round." The grave-digger was at work in the roadside cemetery. "That's where my missus was buried. I'll join her one day," said the farmer, without a trace of emotion.

Unlike Austwick, the village of Clapham had become part of a large estate. The Farrers, whose emblem was the winged horseshoe, had made their "brass" in London, largely through a legal practice controlled by a man of such frugal habits he was known as Penny Bun Oliver. Their debut in the Clapham area came with the purchase of shooting rights on Ingleborough. They bought up property and land in the 19th century. A building frenzy developed. They pretty well re-built the place.

Farrer brass and the brawn of local workmen led to the damming of Clapdale. It not only prettified the estate but allowed water to flow to local taps. A turbine was purchased and soon there was electric lighting in the street and at some of the principal houses. I had been lodging at Wood Cottage when electricity from t'grid was being used in the houses and locally-generated electricity still fitfully illuminated the streets.

At teatime, my host, having consulted his clock several times, pulled a lever and we saw with relief the needle of an enormous dial had been activated. The turbine was operating. The lights were so poor that after dark a sense of mystery remained. When t'grid electric was installed in a cottage, an old widow was heard to complain that "they've putten it in a glass bottle. I can't turn it down or blow it out."

When I first knew Clapham, it was an introverted community – a place of twitching curtains as the residents of two rows of houses and cottages kept tabs on each other across a beck which had five assorted bridges and a resident pair of kingfishers. Farrer enterprise was evident wherever I looked. A Dales church of modest size became something akin to a mini-cathedral. Even the name was changed from St Michael to St James, in deference to one of the Farrer children. (Matthew, the other son, had already been immortalised through the name of the new church at the moor-edge settlement of Keasden).

A farmhouse had blossomed as Ingleborough Hall, with a fine pillared hall, a curving staircase with wondrous iron railings and fireplaces that had been fashioned using a dark limestone in which fossils stood out in contrasting white – this stone being given the grand title of Dent Marble. The grounds of Ingleborough Hall extended over an old right of way, which meant that those using the track had to pass through gloomy tunnels. These ensured that tradesmen might reach the back door without being seen from the principal rooms.

Clapham, on the main road, trembled to the passage of vehicles. Its hitherto god-fearing people became wreckers when a lorry crashed into the beck with a load of tinned food – at a time, just after the Second World War when such items were still being rationed. It was with a shock of horror that the demise of the lorry was reported and nearly all the village came to see it, spread-eagled in the beck-bottom, the area festooned with tins of this and that.

In scenes reminiscent of *Whisky Galore*, Compton Mackenzie's tale

17

of the Hebrides, the tins were removed and dispersed in hidey-holes. Then someone remembered that the policeman was in bed with sciatica – and a few tins were taken to him. The beck water had washed the labels from many of the tins, which meant that at mealtimes there was doubt as to whether a tin contained soup or fruit.

I was driven into a village neatly divided into two by the watercourse that had begun as Fell Beck high on the mountain and became Clapham Beck when it has poured over a cliff near the church. I was to spend the week-end with Harry Scott and his family prior to becoming 33$^1/_3$ of *The Dalesman* staff.

The Scotts lived at a double-fronted house in Gildersbank. Harry had asked the estate agent if he could change the name and permission was forthcoming. The first choice was Beckside, but he thought it might occasionally be represented as Backside. He opted for Fellside. The agent charged 10s a week and said he would have a new bath installed.

The water supply was drawn from the man-made lake and flowed through a mile or two of ancient piping before returning up the side of the village where the Scotts lived. By the time farmers had cooled their milk, and villagers had swilled and gargled, the pressure was low. The Scotts managed to half-fill the bath when they had an unexpected guest – Professor J E M Joad, of *Brains Trust* fame on t'wireless. He had just climbed Ingleborough and was wet, dirty – and hungry.

Harry, a man of moderate height, somewhat sallow complexion and amiable disposition, had moved with his wife Dorothy and two children from Leeds to Clapham in 1934. He freelanced for a while, with sparse returns, and started his homely *Dalesman* magazine in 1939. The first issue, printed by Lamberts of Settle, was hand-set. The bill for several thousand copies was nobbut £25. One operation in this novel cottage industry was loading copies of the latest issue of *Dalesman* into 9 x 6 envelopes. We formed a small group around the fire, chatting as we worked. Dorothy Scott kept up a steady supply of coffee and biscuits.

During a walk through a village where almost everyone was locally-born, cow-claps on the roads hinted at the large bovine population. Clapham was smothered in trees and shrubs. Grannie Cross had a garden that contained so many plants that when she acquired another she had to take one of the existing plants out to make room. This happened when she went on a bus trip to some stately home. Grannie was accompanied by her trusty umbrella, into which she slipped cuttings that had been surreptitiously removed.

Hetty Turner, who had taken me as a lodger for a short time, until the new teacher arrived, lived in a house in which paraffin was the fuel for lighting, heating and cooking. There was a permanent blue-grey haze. I was there in winter, when frost painted pictures on the bedroom window. Leaving my bed in the morning, enticed into the big world by the tang of frying bacon, my bare feet rested on – bare linoleum.

Of the local characters, Ben Hudson, was easily riled. Being short of stature, he was in the habit of standing his horse beside a wall. He would then clamber on to the wall, which he would use as a mounting block. Before he could slip into the saddle, the horse would have moved away, upset by the thought of work. Twice a day, Ben straddled a three-legged stool and, having turned his cap so that the neb was at the back, he coaxed milk from the laden teats. It swished against the sides of a pail. The tail of the cow was apt to swish across his face. If the milker was caught by a muck-button [dry dung, lodged in the hair of the tail] there was a howl like a demented cat.

Hygiene was not an important matter then. The milk was supposed to be passed through a cooler, a metal appliance over which the milk flowed, its temperature being lowered by a flow of cold water within. One of Ben's pals refused to use a cooler though he had to buy one to conform with the regulations. When an inspector called, and saw the shiny appliance, he complimented the farmer on its condition. Said the inspector: "It looks just like new." Which, of course, it was.

For a time, a war-zone existed between Ben Hudson's farmyard, complete with free-range hens, and Jack Winton's vegetable garden, where the hens were prone to feed. Ben, aware that in the garden the hens had a goodly supply of fresh greens, did not rush to repair the intervening fence.

Jack quietly remarked: "If I were you, I'd keep those hens at home." "Why?" said the excited Ben. "Because I'm going to use some weed-killer. It won't do the hens any good," remarked Jack.

Where diplomacy had failed, practical considerations won the day. The fence was repaired.

2 – At Home in Austwick

I reached Cuckoo Town in the most satisfying way – on foot. The route from Clapham led over stiles and through what seemed like endless fields. Wheatears, jaunty little birds newly arrived from their wintering grounds in North Africa, played hide-and-seek, dodging behind the capstones of the wall.

From the freshest cow-claps, in days before everything was drenched by noxious chemicals, came buzzing hordes of blue-bottles.

Sheep stared at me with eyes as ancient-looking as the grey rocks about them before continuing their ancient task of green-keepers. A third of their (to me) boring lives would be spent eating, a third chewing the cud and a third sleeping. They scattered hard brown pellets to compensate the land for the goodness they were taking from it.

In due course, from one of the lynchets [hillside ploughing terraces, created long ago], I beheld Cuckoo Town and its guardian hills. The most prominent from this angle was Oxenber, its old wooded state preserved because tree-felling had been frowned upon. Those seeking fuel used dead or lying wood.

Jimmy-Johnny, a local farmer, was inspecting cattle in a field that sloped gently down to a row of ancient cottages and to a large modern house which the residents had named Yore House, from their old farmstead home at the head of Wensleydale. The drivers of delivery vans wondered why people looked bemused when they asked the way to Yore House. What business had the man with them?

Jimmy-Johnny was a lile chap, like many of the family to which he belonged. Being one of twins who were much alike, the local people were inclined to run the two Christian names together. Jimmy (or was it Johnny) stood in a pony-drawn tub-cart that resembled a chariot. Indeed, he might have been a Roman emperor reviewing his troops rather than a Dales farmer with cattle in mind.

Such men as Jimmy-Johnny spent most of their time and their "brass" on farm stock. Their somewhat shabby appearance and the austere state of rooms at home belied the fact that, in truth, they were well-off. One Austwick farmer, chided about his reticence to spend money, was told: "When thou's gone [died] thy lad'll go through thi money in next-to-no-time." Said the farmer: "If t'lad gits as much pleasure out o' spending brass as I've had makkin' it, he'll be all right."

I heard in the village that Johnny (or was it Jimmy?) was haggling over the price of a cow at the auction mart when his brother sidled up to him and whispered: "Have you got it bought?" "No." An edge had crept in to the brother's voice when he said: "Well, hurry up – I've just selled it!"

The Austwick community had its elite, but there was no cow-towing, if you will excuse the expression, by the farm folk, quarrymen, shopkeepers and tradesmen. When a posh visitor passed a road-sweeper, without even glancing in his direction, the sweeper was heard to say: "If yon chap knew how little I thought of him – he'd speak!" Miss Christabel Ingilby, the nearest we had to aristocracy, talked posh (in comparison with the rough dialect of some) but was respected because "she's no edge."

Miss Ingilby was nice to everybody. She who was born at the big house, Harden, lived to see the family fortune frittered away and was spending her later days in what had been the gardeners' cottage. When asked by a caller if she had any rummage for a forthcoming sale, she replied: "Rummage? I wear mine!"

My first job in Austwick enabled me to meet many more of the villagers. I was one of a quartet of bearers of the coffin at the funeral of someone I had never met. Funerals were not common in a village where people, like old soldiers, did not die but simply faded away. If they managed to clear seventy, they were likely to reach ninety. By that time, Will Pritch would say: "I reckon t'Almighty must have forgotten 'em." None of the chapel-goers died. They "passed over Jordan." The rest of the villagers were "tekken."

John Middleton, the local joiner and undertaker, recruited me and happily it was a fine day. We had a long walk from the church to the burial ground, with four of us pushing the church bier. I heard the unlikely tale of a man who said he would like to be buried just inside the cemetery gate so he'd be "first out" on the Day of Resurrection.

More amusing was the story of the farmer's wife, a "reight natterer." When she died, peace descended on the house. On the funeral day, the coffin was being carried down the stairs from the best bedroom by father and his sons when it collided with an obstruction. From the jolted coffin came a faint cry. They opened it. The wife was not dead after all.

She lived for a year or two, nattering and arguing, and then died once again. As the coffin was being borne down the flight of steps for a second time, the anxious husband said to his sons: "Go easy, lads."

Living in the main street of Austwick were Will and Sally Pritchard, together with Horace, their son, who alas was subject to fits, which he might throw at any time. Sally was a "chitterer" whose mission was going round the village "cheering people up". Sometimes her presence had the opposite effect. She visited a young lady who was about to have a baby and commented: "You'll be capped before it's finished." She was right. It was a big baby that played hard to get.

An expectant mother at Southwaite, one of two farms in Crummack Dale, found herself alone in the house when the birth was imminent. Fortunately, an old lady who lived in Wharfe came to see her at that time and she hastened down to Stanley Harrison's farmhouse at Dear Bought, where there was a telephone. She summoned both midwife and doctor.

Those were the days when most births occurred at home and when – in preparation – sheets of newspaper were laid on the floor. The bed was overspread with newspaper, which was then covered with a waterproof sheet and, in turn, by a cotton sheet. Water was boiled so that the doctor could sterilise his instruments. In the case of Southwaite, the mother-to-be had hardly time to get into bed before the baby was born.

3 - Mrs Bee

Her real name was Maud Bacon. She was a close friend of the Scotts and had agreed to "put me up" during my first weeks with *The Dalesman*. Mrs Bee had a lively, bustling manner that belied her age – middle age, that is. Most people of her generation were now grey-haired but she retained her natural auburn colouring.

She lived at a house called Rothbury, which hinted at her Northumbrian background. I half-expected one of the old Dales houses, complete with mullion windows and with a datestone of the 17th century above a porched door. What I found was a 1930s semi-detached house. The remarkable Mrs Bee and her family had moved here from Leeds at the beginning of the Second World War and adapted so well to rural life that she stayed here when her family had left and through her ownership of a third of an acre of land put in a strong bid for independence, keeping a pig and three hives of bees and some hens.

There was one "hen incident" that Mrs Bee knew nothing about. The family dog got into the hen run and had a lively time chasing hens. One of the birds died and a local lady advised that the dog might be cured of its hen-chasing if the body was tied round its neck. "It was awful but it worked and he never so much as looked at a hen again." A family friend took the dead hen and boiled it for a long time and, presumably, ate it. She did buy a replacement. It must have been a good match. Mrs Bee never seemed to notice.

The notion of an ordinary householder keeping a pig dated from the recent war. Snipping coupons out of ration books was scarcely necessary in an area where farm produce continued to be plentiful. Pork, along with butter, eggs, rabbits, hares, geese and owt else that could be reared or processed filled the local bellies and was part of a distribution system that operated, as in the best detective stories, under cover of night. It also meant less work for the busy staff in the food office at the Town Hall.

An inn just over the hill from Austwick had a sagging roof from the quantity of pig-meat hanging from beams and rafters. In summer, a lad was sent up into the loft daily to ensure the pork was not becoming fly-blown, though the meat did not linger long. Much of it went down the gullets of policemen partial to ham and eggs, one reason why there not many prosecutions for breaking the food laws. Up-country, an inn-keeper became a patron of the arts. One painting, when lifted down, was found to be covering a cupboard stuffed with rationable foodstuffs.

Mrs Bee had abided by the regulations. The pig in her sty was visible to anyone who cared to look over the garden wall. On the farms, during the war and its aftermath, when rationing of food continued for a while, pigs were born, ate, slept, ate again and eventually died with a degree of secrecy that would have aroused the admiration of MI5. Having crammed [over-fed] a pig with oatmeal patties and some flake maize to give the bacon a nice taste, the farmer – first ensuring there was an "r" in the month – summed a pig-killer to perform the last rites.

Pig-killing was a time of gluttony for the farm folk and their friends. The blood was "catched" and used for black puddings. The head was converted into brawn, which in the cooking process had an unpleasant smell but, served cold, was generally considered to be delicious. The dismembered animal was distributed, with attendant winks and nods, in nondescript brown paper packets. The fatty bacon helped to sustain the farm folk in their gruelling daily round. One chap liked to eat bacon "when t'fat's running out of both sides of my mouth."

At the time I lodged with Mrs Bee, rationing had ended. The pig in the garden was the last she would keep. It did ensure that my introduction to Mrs Bee's household was dramatic. Having ended the day's work at *The Dalesman*, and having walked across the fields to my new "digs" at Austwick, I was invited to sit down to a hot meal of distinction. I had no sooner picked up knife and fork than we heard the voice of Hilda, a neighbour: "The pig's got out!"

The meal was forgotten as we went to recapture it before it could snuffle its way across the hallowed croquet lawn. The sty was no pigly Colditz. Part of the enclosure was of brick and part consisted of wire fencing that had been fettled up so often, with so much extra wire, it would have taken a month of concentrated effort to unravel it. When the pig had been imprisoned once again, we added yet more wire to the fence and returned to a meal which was long past its best.

Summer evenings were spent playing croquet. Hours of croquet extended into dusk, when it was difficult to distinguish the colour of a ball. If the bees were lively, the game was inclined to be fitful. All but Mrs Bee rushed while crossing the main flight-lines of nectar-gathering bees. Once or twice during that hot summer, a hive seemed to boil over as bees swarmed. Help was at hand in the form of John Middleton, who apart from being a local joiner and undertaker was an experienced bee-keeper. He had the right temperament for looking after bees, being calm in all circumstances.

I would don a netted hat and some gloves so I could watch the recovery of the swarm. John and Mrs Bee did this using a straw skep, holding it in place on the apple tree where a brown, syrupy mass of bees lay. A quick shake, and the bulk of them were in the skep, which was then laid on the ground so all might join the Queen.

In the late evening, the swarm was transferred to an empty hive. I watched the regal progress of the Queen up a running board and saw with what devotion the rest of the bee community attended her. Part of this dark brown army of insects took a route that lay over Mrs Bee's feet, which were encased in floppy sandals. Mrs Bee, not wanting any of the bees to be injured, picked them up gently, one by one, and re-routed them. I was assured they would not sting. "They're sated with honey."

The most feared colony of bees in the village was owned by Norman

Burniston and were known as "the Austwick tigers." These bees stung for the fun of it. Rouse them, as when trying to get at their spare honey, and they stung so freely exposed parts of your body would have affinities with a pin cushion.

The worst incident occurred one summer evening when John Middleton was helping Norman to remove part of a hive.

The top part fell, not far but with a sharp enough impact to put the Austwick tigers in a thoroughly bad mood. They were especially skilled at finding entry points on head-nets. Norman, screaming that he was being murdered, dashed into the house and wrapped an eiderdown, plus a few dozen bees, round his head. John and I stared, with drooping lower jaws, as pandemonium reigned in the bedroom. We had a clear view from a high part of the garden. Then we heard the sound of a sneck being lifted and a woman's voice. Mother, aged ninety or there-abouts, was returning from the Women's Institute meeting. She switched on the electric light. Bees that had settled down in the gloom for the night, buzzed around it. Both mother and son had a fitful night and they left the windows open so the remaining "tigers" could leave the house at first light. Neither mother or son would ever suffer from rheumatism again if the bee-sting remedy was to be believed.

Mrs Bee had the old-fashioned belief that the Devil has work for idle hands. She contrived to remain busy from before dawn until after dusk. When the work in house and garden was done, she tested her wits against the compiler of the crossword in *The Yorkshire Post*. Or coaxed me and others to join her in card games of interminable length, using a shuffler, a device she had bought while visiting her brother in America. The pack of cards was divided into two, placed on opposite sides of the little appliance, a wheel was turned and the cards were neatly inter-leaved.

A devout churchwoman, Mrs Bee defended Anglican tradition against any modernist tendencies on the part of the vicar, who held his views with equal tenacity. An enthusiastic member of the Women's Institute she made jam and sang *Jerusalem* and listened intently to talks about soft-toy making, cookery and embroidery. A traditionalist, Mrs Bee maintained the Headingley traditions, such as Elevenses, a formal ritual, conducted in the sitting-room with Edwardian splendour.

This room, like the British Empire, had about it a faded glory. Talk tended to range over serious matters. Wisecracks would have been inappropriate against a background of antique furniture and heavily patterned wallpaper. Wooden objects carved by an uncle during the fretwork craze adorned the room. Several musical boxes, bought during family holidays in Switzerland, included one that resembled a piece of carved wood. Anyone who surreptitiously lifted it out of curiosity were startled to hear a tinkling tune.

The ladies of Mrs Bee's coterie were mainly spinsters and widows, some of awesome intelligence. Mrs Todd, Miss Whittaker, Mrs Crompton and the others extended their interests beyond the local

preoccupation with the weather, livestock, lunch or where the next penny was coming from.

Elevenses was taken seriously and involved wearing the best setting-off clothes. If there were children in train, they must be well-disciplined children. One widow was so small, so thin, I entertained the thought that when she had drunk a cup of tea, she would resemble a thermometer.

The focal point of the room was a cake-stand, the various levels packed with delicacies. A villager would have described the sandwiches as being so dainty "it takes three at a time to fill thee gob." The guests sipped tea, which was poured from a teapot that had been pre-warmed. The tea leaves had an unfamiliar taste. I had been brought up on Co-op tea and an inter-war jingle about "a nice cup of tea in the morning," etc.

We deftly handled crumbly scones, binding them with generous applications of butter before transferring them to our mouths. We were keen to know more about the ingredients, suspecting that they were home-laid or home-grown. And so they were. Mrs Bee's garden yielded eggs, honey, fresh green, berries for jam-making.

Her visitors provided never-failing topics of interest, not only in the household but throughout the larger family – the village. A dainty little nonagenarian who stayed a few days was fully-fashioned, with permed hair and clothes of the latest style. She puffed her way through a dozen cigarettes a day and incinerated a few more when in bed where, clad in silk pyjamas, and propped up by a pillow, she read the latest crime novels.

As for me, lodging with Mrs Bee, fresh-air fanatic, through a frosty winter, I habitually slept in a bedroom with the windows wide open and without a hot-water bottle. I was permitted to have some hot milk laced with rum when I had a really bad cold.

4 – Round and About

Life in Cuckoo Town was never dull. Most of the residents had been born locally. None was widely travelled, except those who had their overseas trips paid for by the King when they were on military service. On one of my early getting-to-know-you walks I encountered Nathan Booth when he was hand-milking a cow. He winced, touched an aching tooth and promptly went indoors to remove it with a pair of pliers. Nathan resumed his milking, winced again and said: "I've pulled t'wrong tooth." And he returned indoors to do something about it.

An old chap in the main street occupied just the ground floor room of his cottage, spending most of his days and all his nights sitting in a chair, which was the single item of furniture, looking at a few glowing coals and surrounded by bags full of the rakings of previous fires – plus a reserve of fuel.

We had our priorities right. Marjorie, a gentle lady who was keen on botany, would never refer to the bloody cranesbill and thought whoever named it should have chosen a more seemly title. To her, it was the rose-red cranesbill. One Springtime afternoon she ran after me, arrived breathless and full of excitement. What had happened? An accident? Illness? Said Marjorie, her eyes shining: "I've just seen the first colts-foot."

It was Frederic Riley, Marjorie's father, who told me about Cuckoo Town as it was in the 1930s. He was a kindly soul who lived in Settle but commuted by Pennine bus to the bottom of Rawlinshaw Brow, which he ascended, in all types of weather. He then followed a winding road, between drystone walls, that led to Stockdale Cottage, at the highest part of Feizor. This little hamlet was tucked away in a fold among the quiet hills. Here, Fred (as I usually thought of him) pottered about in the garden. Or he sorted out lantern slides of the old glass type – the type that

31

fell with a resounding *clunk* into the carrier of what was generally known as a "magic lantern."

Fred Riley's main occupation was engine-driver at a local mill, which partly explains why he was in love with Nature. When the mill hooter had signalled the end of the working day, his mind switched to Zion, the chapel beneath the scars at Settle where he had been married in 1905. Zion throve to the extent that Fred was able to form an orchestra that gave concerts to packed congregations after the evening services. Sometimes, a piece of limestone from Castleberg trundled down the hill. There would come a time when an anxious pastor would go to an insurance company about the matter, only to be told: "Sorry, we can't insure it. If a rock hit the chapel we would regard it as an Act of God."

Fred's support of religion did not wane when he took his two children on holiday at the seaside. They were keen to make sand-castles on the beach but the first evening was spent looking for a suitable place of worship to attend on Sunday morning. When Sunday came, they must act with decorum and not think of playing games. Marjorie, his daughter, by now desperate to get on to the beach, asked: "Will you let us go there with our buckets and spades if we build sand-chapels, not sand-castles?"

When Fred Riley was not in his best suit at chapel, he might be seen cycling about the district with a full-plate camera and accessories strapped to the pillion. The photographic plates he exposed were converted into lantern slides. Having been born at Preston, where the mighty Ribble was stung by salt water, Fred concentrated first on a lantern-lecture entitled *The Ribble from its Source to the Sea*, a theme which was also converted into book form.

In his twilight years, Fred and his wife had a bookshop at Settle. He retired from giving slide shows in 1953. One day, while sitting with him in his little hillside cottage at Feizor, and looking out over an old-fashioned flower garden, he recalled for me episodes of his life and also what he considered to be the great days of magic lantern shows. He had used hand-tinted slides made from his own photographs. As he spoke, I recalled one such show, at which the audience clapped at some of the more colourful pictures which today would be considered lurid.

His first shows were presented at a time when none of the Dales halls had electricity. If there was a supply of gas, a flexible pipe could be led off to the lantern to join forces on a column of lime with a stream of oxygen from a rope-protected cylinder on the floor. An acetylene lamp burned so hot that during its trials the lantern had to be removed from the hall on a shovel. Fred devised a lantern with a paraffin lamp as the light source, but the image on the screen was so poor it was, to quote out of context from the Good Book, like looking through a glass darkly.

Another time, his request for a pointer, with which he could indicate interesting features of his pictures, was met with an unusual response. The caretaker handed him a broom, with the business end still attached. At a primary school, a child brought him a jam jar full of water and said he had just taken the minnows out of it. A door-keeper barred his way and when Fred said he was the lecturer he was told that story would not wash. "Sorry," said the doorman. "I've already let one lecturer in."

At his old cottage in Feizor, Fred – good Christian that he was – wrote about a world in which goodness was taken for granted and it was always sunny. His sweet-sounding phrases should have been set to organ music. When it came to describing Austwick, he "confessed to a feeling of pleasurable anticipation." In short, the place was romantic. "The majority of the houses form part of Austwick's somewhat straddling street, where ancient and modern examples mingle promiscuously, with the result that there is no particular portion that is exclusively old, nor any part entirely modern."

He mentioned past industrial enterprises. At Austwick, spinning, hand-loom weaving and sometimes knitting augmented the income from farming. "Austwick spinners had a reputation for producing good work. Manufacturers as far afield as Halifax sent their wool tops to be spun by the villagers. The wool was carried by packhorses, a small shop-keeper acting as agent, and paid a halfpenny a pound for receiving and distributing the wool." A derelict building opposite the village cross was still known as the Weaving Shed.

Austwick Mill, which stood on a bank of Wharfe Beck, was offered for sale in the 1830s, being described as having "a powerful stream of water from 30 to 40 ft fall. These premises are worthy of attention of any person desirous of entering on the Spinning and Manufacturing Business." Not long afterwards, the property burnt down. The new mill, built across the road from where t'old mill had stood, was used for sawing flagstones, taking water from the same source as its predecessor. The Silurian flags used extensively for cisterns and floor covering came chiefly from Dry Rigg Quarry on Swarthmoor. In the 1930s, there were still folk who referred to the bridge carrying the road across Wharfe Beck as "Saw Mill Brigg."

In 1937, Austwick received the blessings of electricity and, wrote Fred, "the fact was proclaimed in a very obvious fashion. Nevertheless, in spite of unlovely poles and overhead wires, electricity has proved a real boon, some of the old houses now being better lighted on a winter's night than during the brightest of summer days."

On a good day, Fred might extend his walk into Crummack Dale, the source of the beck that flowed by Wharfe, writing that its waters, "after tumbling in little cascades through Kickersgill, pursue a leisurely course along the ever-broadening valley." Crummack Farm, near the head of the dale, was occupied in fairly recent times by the Brown family, who had been at remote little Cosh, one and a-half miles beyond the head of Littondale.

Mrs Brown had been known at Cosh to invite passing ramblers into the house for a cup of tea so she could get some news of the outer world. The postman called because she had ordered *The Yorkshire Post,* copies of which were to be posted to her. A visitor to Crummack Farm at the time she was ill heard Mrs Brown say that the only time she got away from the farm and met other people was when she had her babies. She arranged for them to be born at a nursing home.

Crummack Dale, with its beds of Silurian rock capped at the edges by limestone, was a happy hunting ground for -ologists, mainly geologists. "Now and again a contingent of young campers swept down on the village like a little avalanche and display in their new-found freedom an exuberance of spirits calculated to startle some of the older inhabitants."

Indeed. The *rap, rap* of geological hammers sounded like the drumming of a race of demented woodpeckers. Farmers like Mr Booth took a dim view of -ologists who rove pieces of rock from the landscape and "napped" them in one of his best meadows just before haytime. A happier consequence of the visits of young college folk was that some of the lasses married local lads bringing, through their progeny, some fresh blood into a somewhat jaded rural stock.

5 – Yew Tree Cottage

Freda and I were married at East Marton in September, 1952, and spent our honeymoon at Oban. A supplementary wedding present was given to us by the ticket-collector on the train we boarded at Skipton. The third-class compartments were full so we trespassed on first-class, offering to pay the difference. The collector looked at the litter of confetti on the floor and put away his "clipper." No extra charge would be made.

Our first accommodation after marriage was the front room and a bedroom at Mrs Bee's, which we could use until we had our own accommodation. Our first true home was one of a row of cottages just across the road. It was referred to locally as Methody Row because the owner was a devout Methodist and, though he did not put it in so many words, the three cottages were let to folk of Methodist persuasion. Apart from ourselves, they were old people, kindly people, but so far gone down the road of life the next resting place was the cemetery.

A cottage became vacant when a retired Methodist minister died. His widow decided to migrate to warmer climes. He had been ailing for years but retained a capacity for lucid thought, through which ran a thin vein of humour. I asked him to contribute an article to a chapel magazine I was editing. This Methodist scholar, the author of several theological books, leapt at the chance to express himself, though he lacked the capacity to write. He dictated an article to me and it was recorded using Mr Pitman's shorthand.

I used the interview verbatim, including his story of how the stewards of Cowling chapel, when meeting them for the first time, had regarded them critically. Then one remarked: "We reckon your wife will be a singer. She has legs like a sparrow." This did not please the wife, but in her widowhood she cannot have borne me a grudge for it was she who told me about her impending departure from Yew Tree Cottage.

I scuttered across the road from Mrs Bee's house to ask the landlord, Handby Ewbank, if I could rent the place. My credentials were good. There was Methodism in my madness. I was, indeed, a "locust" preacher, as one of the villagers called the voluntary band of part-time workers. A neighbour told her she was mistaken. "They're local preachers. A locust is something that arrives and eats up all before it." The villager said: "That's what one preacher did when he had tea at our house."

The meeting between landlord and prospective tenant was affable, except that on that November evening all the elements combined to make it physically uncomfortable. As I stood chatting with Handby at his back door, a wind full of spite threw handfuls of snow at me. There was I, under-dressed and carpet-slippered, on a draughty doorstep, discussing the serious matter of rent and conditions of tenancy.

At a vulnerable stage, when I was full of gratitude, Handby asked me if I would help with hay-making next year. Of course I would. In any case, haytime seemed light years ahead. Which is why, ten minutes later – or so it seemed – I was reminded of my promise. And why, on the sunniest weeks of the following seven years, when I should have been out walking with my wife and growing family, I laboured in the hayfield for the princely wage of – nowt.

In truth, I gained things that were much more valuable than brass. Handby was a good friend and fellow chapelgoer. Haytiming was a healthy occupation, undertaken in air that was at times tinglingly fresh. I gained an insight into the many haytime jobs at a time before the machines took it over, leading (though no one knew it at the time) to stuffing wilted grass into black plastic bags, a row of which was to be described by the driver of a tourist coach as "a black pudding factory."

I made the acquaintance of an old-time farmer called Frank Lambert. When we broke off work for the hayfield meal known as "drinkings," he regaled me with tales from his youth. He'd been employed by a stingy farmer who didn't want to see farm men in the house except at meal or bed times. In deepest winter, Frank used to go into the shippon and warm his hands on the backs of the cows. When a cow was ill, the pre-scribed remedy was akin to black-magic.

One chap inquired of a friend at the auction mart what he had given the cow that had a stomach disorder. "Paraffin," he replied. Some months later, the two men met again. The man who had asked about the remedy said to the other: "I gave my cow some paraffin – and she died." The first man commented: "Aye, lad – and so did mine!" As told by Frank, with a crinkling of the face, it sounded like a stock joke.

When Peggy, Frank's faithful horse, departed (to the abattoir, I discovered much later), Handby had horse-power in the form of a Ferguson tractor – a "lile grey Fergie." It was on it that I picked up the rudiments of driving a mechanical vehicle, especially the care needed when releasing the clutch when there was a trailer loaded with hay and, on top, a man with a sharp-pronged fork.

Freda and I took over a cottage that, outside, was good enough to grace a picture postcard and, within, was, as one might expect, bleak

38

and bare. The centre of the living room was a meeting place for half a dozen eager draughts, for there were three doors and two windows, one being of the wide variety, mullioned and dripstoned in the Dales style. The path leading up to a central door was cobbled and shaded by a large, well-trimmed yew tree. Hence the name Yew Tree Cottage.

That is not the name by which the Council knew the property. When we received our first rate demand, the official name of our cottage was revealed as Spouts Croft. The spout appeared in an outbuilding, then went to ground again and took a course that provided watering places for livestock in several fields. Before I realised this, I had washed a watering can there, having just used it to spread some noxious liquid on the garden weeds. The dilution of what remained must have been considerable, yet when I next walked down Orcaber Lane I glanced anxiously into the fields, hoping there would be no cows on their backs, legs in the air, indicating sudden death.

Above the front door of the cottage was an electric light, a vital feature if anyone visiting us on a winter evening was to negotiate the cobbles without tripping. The light also revealed that a robin roosted in a shrub beside the door. On a frosty night, when greeting or bidding farewell to friends, I would glance at the bush to assure myself that the robin had gone to bed.

Yew Tree Cottage was set into a hillside. From the front door a flight of steps led to two bedrooms and a bathroom. The kitchen window and the back window of the living room were fitted with iron bars so that cows ambling up to the window, and looking down on us as we dined, were not able to join us. Freda's father, a retired farmer, was delighted to be able to judge Jimmy-Johnny's stock from the comfort of a fireside chair, though he occasionally wandered up the field to a recumbent cow and, as it rose, rear end first, ran his hand over its back, the tail-root and bag to judge its quality. He was also able to assess its value to a pound or two.

Most of the floor was flagged and our first job was to cover the flag-stones with felt, the sort used to roof chicken coops. We never did cure the draught problem. On an evening when the wind had an edge to it like a blade made of Sheffield steel; when the carpet was flapping and the open fire roaring in the draught, visitors did not stay for long, their normal ruddy complexions soon taking on a blueish tinge.

It was at Yew Tree Cottage that our children, David and Janet, were reared. Each was born in springtime. When the first feed of the day took place, we opened the bedroom windows wide to let in truly fresh air. A vibrant dawn chorus of birds, in those days, seemed to make that air shiver. Later, from the windows, we could look over  Mrs Bee's garden to see a bright golden haze on the meadows.

At Mrs Bee's, the croquet season began at Easter, with the ritualistic re-painting of the wooden balls, and it ended with the first frosts of autumn, by which time the season for card games such as Canasta had returned. On sunlit evenings, when croquet was in vogue, we sometimes avoided showing ourselves at our front windows, even moving on all-fours. Otherwise, we would hear the ringing voice of Mrs Bee, inviting us to join her in the garden, where a croquet party was assembling. With croquet, one could have too much of a good thing.

On a mundane level, we had the chimney cleaned. Mr Young of Giggleswick was summoned. He rode over Buckhaw Brow on his trusty bike, which was draped with his chimney-cleaning tackle – rods, cloths and the circular brush with the stiff hairs. Looking at it, I imagined fancifully that it had just had a fright. Despite his advanced years, Mr Young was tall and lish, also laconic of speech. He did not believe in using two words if one would do. He had elevated the pregnant silence into an art form.

The children, now at the toddler stage, looked wide-eyed as the chimney sweep prepared for action, using a soot-impregnated cloth to cover the fireplace and to restrict to the grate the expected deluge of soot. He then screwed the brush on to a rod and introduced it to the chimney, twisting and pushing as one length of rod was attached to another.

Freda produced a mug of tea. He drank some of it. Then, turning to the wide-eyed children, he uttered his longest sentence of the day: "Shall I put you on t'brush and shove you up t'chimla?" The children did not stay long enough to provide an answer, though they were friends of Mr Young again when he invited them to go into the garden and keep their eyes on the chimney, reporting to him when t'brush appeared to view.

We had an unpaid handyman called Jack Swale. He worked for the Rural Council but readily assisted us with technical problems, such as those accruing when, having made up a set of kitchen cabinets, I found the kitchen door too narrow to admit the largest of them. One Christmas, having bought a train set for our young son, we decided to assemble it the evening before to ensure it was in working order. The only other train set of that type in the village had been bought by Harry Lord who, indeed, had ordered the set that now reposed in our Glory Hole, waiting for December 25th.

On Christmas Eve, with Jack in attendance, we unpacked the present and set about connecting the tracks to form the traditional circuit. One by one the sleepers of the tracks snapped. And so it was that, an hour or two before Santa Claus was due, Jack set about welding the pieces together. The train was operational during Christmas Morning, though when Harry Lord's son arrived and we asked about his set, he replied: "Its broken. Dad's going to buy me an electric set – next Christmas."

Jack performed another service. He taught me how to drive a car. Before that occurred, I used the bus. I would wait at the Clapham bus stop with Jackie Holme, the blacksmith. One wild and wet evening, Jack Swale drew up in his little Council van and offered us a lift to Austwick. Jack drove the van with his usual verve under a leaden sky and through dubs that were almost large enough to be classified as ponds. Sheets of water displaced by the van poured noisily on to the roof. Jack drew up near the bus shelter at Austwick. We clambered out, wobbled a little and I prepared to thank the driver. Jackie Holme said: "And next time, Swale, go by t'bloody road."

Apart from bedroom and dining suites, we had furnished Yew Tree Cottage with our wedding presents. They ranged from a purple vase to a pegged rug made by Grannie, aged ninety-two. It consisted of "mill beatings" and, placed in the bedroom, shielded our bare feet from chilly linoleum. Years later, when Freda decided it must be washed, she took it to a laundrette in Settle, fearing that our washing machine of modest size would get its own version of indigestion if we filled it with a mat. Freda set the larger machine in motion and went shopping. She returned to find, instead of a rug, a grey mush. Hastily she bought a bag, scooped handfuls of mush into it and deposited the bag and the pitiful remains of Grannie's pegged rug, into the nearest litter bin.

The garden had a rockery on which the children loved to sit, watching the world go by, and becoming excited at the approach of Nathan Booth, retired farmer, who would stop and say: "Do you want a toe-toe?" They did. He was offering them toffees. They dutifully reported to Freda what had happened. The toe-toes were usually kept until after lunch.

The side garden had a lawn that had an aversion to looking nice. A botanist friend, entering that yew-shaded patch of ground, stared with horror at a lusty plant that was festooned with large black berries. We had explained to him that the garden was once a botanist's paradise. A Mr Handby kept it and the plants he tended were listed by the topographer Harry Speight in his book about the area. Our friend asked for a spade and sack. He dug up the plant, dumped it in the sack, washed his hands and said we had been harbouring what must surely have been Yorkshire's finest specimen of deadly nightshade.

The cottage, standing near the main road through the village, was a first-rate observation post. I had a small ground-floor study. In daylight hours, no one could pass unnoticed. I would hear a bleating of sheep, a pattering of hard cleaves on tarmac, and see a flock pass with an attendant farmer's wife, complete with stick and brace of collies. Her husband followed behind – in his battered Land Rover. There would be a swish of cycle wheels as a lively octogenarian, one Chris Cheetham, went by on his bike. He was clad in the sort of clothes, including khaki shorts, favoured by a cyclist in the 1920s. Until a few years before, Chris had taken his ninety-year-old mother for a spin on the family tandem.

Stanley Burniston would drive by in his black Humber car, a vehicle that had been built robustly for wartime service and had the stamina of a tank. He kept it out-of-doors in a shady area of the garden. The car never properly dried out. Grass grew on the running boards. Stanley, who lived at The Traddock, frequently drove to Clapham railway station.

One day, as he sped down the hill from Clapham, he failed to negotiate a sharp, right-hand bend near Crina Bottom. The Humber ploughed through a drystone wall and fell several feet into the field. Stanley, uninjured, coolly selected a lower gear and drove the hefty vehicle through an open gate and back on to the road. Later, he rang up the farmer and arranged for the wall to be patched up. The car did not need any garage attention.

More sedate even than Stanley's Humber was an ancient but well-preserved Austin used as a taxi by George Truelove, proprietor of a grocer's shop that was unkindly referred to as the Short Weight Stores. We never found his scales biased towards the shop-keeper, though (as will be related) we stopped buying potato crisps and breakfast cereals that had been in the shop so long they had lost their ability to snap, crackle or pop.

A trickle of visitors to our cottage included James R Gregson, my favourite Yorkshire playwright. He arrived one Sunday morning, when Freda had gone to church and I had been left in charge of a toddler son. Jimmy stayed so long that I overlooked my domestic duties, such as preparing lunch, and the toddler, encouraged by Jimmy, had removed half my books from the shelves round about the room and was standing ankle deep in them.

The man who became famous in his time through radio as well as stage productions had been brought up in a West Riding mill town. The family lived in dire poverty. One Christmas, he told me, mother returned home with a pitiful bundle of parcels – a few currants, a tiny wedge of cheese, and so on. She set the oven going and in due course had made two "measly, miserable loaves" for the Christmas spread. As she set them on the dresser, mother had said, fiercely: "These are for them 'at comes in – understand? You dare ask for a bit, an' I'll skin ye! I'm not havin' you crying poverty!" At mother's funeral, dad and the boys, decked in "new black" out of the insurance money, sat down to a ham-and-tongue tea that made Dick goggle.

He had some glorious expressions, such as "yon chap were so bow-legged he couldn't stop a pig in a ginnel" and, imitating a waspish woman, "never put thee husband on a pedestal; thou'll nobbut have to dust him!"

The front door of Yew Tree Cottage was secured by a Yorkshire sneck, a simple if noisy device. Anyone entering the house had first to lift t'sneck, which worked on a rocker principle that appealed to the Rev W T F Castle when he popped in for a cup of tea and a natter. He had retired to Settle and helped out at local churches, including Austwick. A fresh-air fanatic, he commuted over Buckhaw Brow, in all weathers, on foot. When I stopped my car and offered him a lift, he remarked: "To keep healthy, I walk at least ten miles a day."

On one visit, he told a story concerning a Yorkshire sneck. He had been appointed to the parish of Dalehead in the upper Hodder, long before Stocks reservoir was built. In those days there was an autumn run of salmon. So numerous were the fish that they almost had to queue to get to the headwaters to spawn. Local people used various methods to remove them, a favourite fishing implement being a rake. They were, of course, poaching. Mr Castle, the new vicar, preached a sermon denouncing such behaviour.

On the following day, when he wanted to leave the vicarage, the sneck refused to budge so he went out of the building by another door. Hanging from the front door sneck was a freshly-caught salmon to which was attached a brief note: "Tak it and say nowt." He took the salmon – and could never again bring himself to preach about the evils of poaching.

On another visit, he regaled us with tales of his missionary days in the Canadian Backwoods. He had got on so well with the native folk that he was invested as an honorary chief of a tribe, who awarded him a fine headdress as proof. He was visited by a man from back o' beyond who said that his remote little community was thinking of building a church. When it was finished, would he (Mr Castle) ask the Bishop to perform the opening ceremony? He would.

In due course the Bishop was transported by dog-sled, over thick snow, to a part of his diocese he had never before visited, not even in summer conditions. The wooden church was packed with worshippers. The man who had visited Mr Castle sidled up to him and asked if a collection might be taken. Of course! The man strode jauntily to the front of the church, held out his hat, drew a gun from a holster, and said: "I'm coming round for some cash. Five dollars each – or else!" With a gun representing "or else," the hat filled with notes and IOUs.

At Yew Tree Cottage, we had what the Methodists might call a Glory Hole. In their case, it was the space under the pulpit, a repository for such items as broken chairs and old hymn-boards. The Glory Hole held the foisty smell from old hymn books. Our understairs "hole" formed a useful darkroom as well as a dump. We heard of former tenants who had used it as a bolt-hole. Father, a pillar of t'chapel, was old-fashioned in his ways. He believed that anyone out and about after nine o'clock was "up to no good." This attitude debarred his two daughters from going dancing (which, in any case, was not a pursuit worthy of a Christian. It was the Devil who tango-ed).

When their mother, who was more understanding of the needs of young folk, had tucked the old chap up in bed, she helped them prepare for dancing. There was a flurry of activity as the girls changed their clothes and, shockingly, applied cosmetics. They set off for the parish hall. It was hardly to dance the night away, for dances were on Saturday evenings and the last waltz had to be completed by 11-59 p.m.

One evening, the eldest daughter brought home her new boy friend, who was making his first acquaintance with mother and with Yew Tree Cottage. They moved whisperingly about the house. Yet father awoke. There was the inevitable creaking of floorboards as he prepared to come down to investigate. The new boy friend, already bemused by the whispers and "shushes" in a darkened house, found himself being shoved under t'stairs – a second or two before father, in old-time nightgown and carrying a lighted candle, appeared to view. He was ushered back to bed. The boy friend made his exit by the side door and over the rockery.

Our neighbours were Mrs Handby, an old and kindly soul, and her bachelor brother, Harry Holden, a retired farm man whose special skills were in drystone walling. Harry walked to and from Settle on market day. When he had a distressing skin complaint, his dedicated sister spent an hour or so a day rubbing liniment into his body.

Occasionally, she baby-sat for us, though our social life at Austwick did not exactly buzz. Mrs Handby, having put on one of her better frocks – one with a floral design – arrived at the house precisely on time. Having been brought up under a severe domestic regime, she would go no further than a straight-backed chair that stood just inside the living room and there she would sit, with her back as straight as a broomshaft and with a serene look on her face, as though she was pondering on happy things. When we returned, hours later, there was no detectable change in her posture. The customary supper-on-a-tray remained untouched.

The third cottage in Methody Row was occupied by Mrs Preece, a farmer's widow. As the only young male person in the Row, I had some annual jobs, such as "slacking" a lump of lime and using it to put another coat of whitewash on t'ceiling. Harry told me that whitewashing had been a wet-weather job for Irishmen who were hired to help with haytime. They called it bug-blinding. I also had the task of clearing blocked drains and replacing spent electric bulbs that were of lower power. They lasted for years and, by the time they burnt out, had become encrusted with the stiff bodies of flies.

Memories of Yew Tree Cottage are linked with my possession of a car, a black Ford saloon, c1939. As you will have gathered, it was second-hand in the trading sense but there had been umpteen hands at the wheel. Its glory days were over. I garaged it in a redundant barn owned by Frank Lambert. It took its place beside a typical array of farmer's junk – bits and pieces that "might come in one day" but never did.

When I took it to Simmy Hartley's garage at Clapham, where it must have had an inferior complex in the presence of the latest models, the report of their investigation was not encouraging. My car had tappet-rattle, piston slap, a crack at one side of the chassis – "oh, and the engine should be fastened to the car a bit more firmly than it is."

Yet, in the course of editing two north-country magazines, I drove that car to remote spots and only once did I have a sinking feeling. This happened in Borrowdale where, after incessant rain, the new flooring that had been fitted by a friend at an extremely cheap price began to sag. My seat was big and cumbersome. It was not intended for a Ford car. The result was that I looked down through a widening gap and saw the road passing beneath me. The answer to my dilemma lay at a joiner's shop in Keswick, where good floorboards were fitted – and creosoted – for a few shillings, allowing me to return home.

The only other major problem occurred at Ravenglass, where the exhaust pipe broke into two pieces, which were re-united by Mr Pharoah, at the local garage, who was self-taught, judging by the way he used a hammer to knock in the ends of one piece and then bash it into the other. It was, he said, a job that would last for years. Next day, in North Ribblesdale, with the rain teeming as though from a celestial hosepipe, part of the exhaust fell away.

6 – The Old Hall

Austwick Hall looked spooky even on a summer's day. The place seemed to be in perpetual shadow. I never actually met the owner, who rarely visited the place. My visits were fortnightly, by the cold light of the moon. Owls hooted in the wood. I expected a flypast of bats. Goodness knows what was making the shrubs rustle as I blundered over the flags, then over cobbles, on my way to the back door.

It was a massive door, with a Yorkshire sneck which, when used, sounded down the passage beyond like a thunderclap. There was time, before the door swung open, to notice a carved TRC, the initials of the Victorian owner, Thomas Richard Clapham.

The Squire, as he liked to think of himself, was thin on top but there was compensation in the bush-like beard. He had knocked about the world a bit and, like Darwen, had a scientific approach to what he saw, though he is not credited with devising any theories about the world around us. His passion was in photography, then at an early stage. He experimented with X-rays, photographing one of his hands, complete with a ring, the resultant picture showing the bone structure and the ring to perfection. His macro-photography included a study of the leg of a spider. He was a keen astronomer, with an observatory in the garden. Goodness knows what he did in the cellar, if such existed.

In short, Thomas Richard Clapham was a character – a person of original thought and action. He certainly left his mark on Austwick Hall and local peaks, branding his initials into woodwork and using a cold chisel on rocks, including mighty Norber.

My appointment with Austwick Hall was with Arthur Foster, the caretaker, who with his wife ran the whist drives on behalf of the British Legion. Arthur handed me a list of winners so that I could incorporate them in my weekly news submitted to the *Craven Herald*. The winners at successive whist drives varied little.

All I knew about the hall was what I could see during the minute or two the door was open. Then, one evening, I was allowed to peep into the reception hall, which was baronial in its proportions, setting the tone of the place with its oak panelling and pillared staircase, adorned by a figured cast iron balustrade. No one remembered Thomas Richard, but there were still a few ladies who remembered when Mrs Clapham, nee Sarah Byers, presided over a sewing meeting at which garments were made for the poor. Tea, sandwiches and cakes were served at half time. Just before Christmas, Sheila Lovett turned up with her Girl Guides and they sang carols in the hall, which had been seasonally decorated. Ivy entwined the pillars.

I found Austwick Hall less interesting by day. The stonework seemed coarse and dark. The oldest part was reputed to have walls that were seven to eight feet thick. It was said to rest partly on an ice-borne block of Silurian rock, similar to the erratics, those famous perched boulders on the slopes of Norber. Previous owners had not left a mark here. Generations of folk – Yorkes, Ingilbys and Farrers – had come and gone. The Hall became the property of the Claphams of Feizor in 1846 and Thomas Richard Clapham inherited it in 1863. His collection of lantern slides came into my possession, having been sold when the Clapham link was severed and handed on until they came to Mrs Green, of Bradley, who thought I would be interested in them.

They create an astonishing picture of a well-to-do Victorian family – father, mother (one of three sisters, each tall and angular, with square jaws), Noel, Richard and Anne. Here is a study of Jack Foster, the pig killer, who also supplied meat to navvies working on the Settle-Carlisle, which transformed the appearance of North Ribblesdale in the 1870s. Jack also played the fiddle at local dances. Another picture was of Jimmy Capstick, blacksmith, with Jessie, his black pony, the other pony belonging to the family being named Dandy. They hauled a phaeton to and from Clapham station.

Henry Shepherd, bearded like so many of his contemporaries, was one of the villagers who posed before the squire's big plate camera. It was Henry, with local help, who had converted a barn into a parish hall. Yet another photograph was of Bird Dick and his wife Betty, portrayed in the garden of Battle Hill. Bird Dick caught finches and coaxed them into song. His wife was known as Bird Betty to distinguish her from two other Betty Wilsons, known as Dearbought Betty, from the name of her farm, and Betty-in-the-Fold.

Thomas Richard died in 1911. Sarah wore "widow's weeds," these being a cap and dark full-length dress. When she died in the springtime during the 1920s, a servant, knowing of her love for primroses, picked a bunch and placed them in a bowl which was set in the room where her body lay in state. The coffin was conveyed to Clapham on the bier that her late husband had given to Austwick Church. It was the first time the bier had been used.

The profligacy of their two sons was a major cause of the Clapham family losing the Hall and estate. It turned out to be a matter of "easy come, easy go." Their eldest son, Richard, was apprenticed by his father to a firm of Leeds architects but, losing interest, he did not take the intermediate examination. The annoyed father gave the lad some money and hinted that he might go to one of the Colonies. Richard took ship to Canada, married an older lady who had nursed him during an illness. She gave him a divorce, whereupon he returned home – and, to father's anguish, married a publican's daughter. Richard now took up a sporting life in Lakeland. He wrote about it in books and articles.

Noel, his brother, had the misfortune to have a "droopy mouth," which made him look miserable. He, too, liked the sporting life and was married twice, his first wife being related to Richard Brinsley Sheridan, the Irish playwright. Their sister, Annie, was educated at home and had a Swedish governess. Richard and Noel would occasionally turn up at Austwick for a few days' sport among the grouse and rabbits. Valiant efforts were made to keep the garden in good order. When special visitors were due, Annie left the house by the kitchen door, climbed six steps and turned a wheel, allowing water to flow to a fountain in the garden. Oil lamps provided illumination in the house. Ellen and Bessie, two servants, had candles to light the way as they climbed over 50 steps to the attic room where they slept. (The steps had to be scrubbed clean every fortnight).

When it became necessary for Austwick Hall to be sold, Annie moved into lodgings in the Lake District. She was still very much alive in the 1950s, when we lived in the village.

7 – The Ladies of Harden

The bluest blood in Austwick coursed through the veins of Miss Christabel Ingilby who, as though you needed to be reminded, was a descendant of the Ingilbys of Lawkland Hall.

Miss Ingilby – we *never* used her Christian name – did not live in such a grand building as the Hall. Her branch of the family had moved to Harden, a former dower house that was at the edge of Austwick. To me, it was like Manderley, the house that had fascinated the novelist Daphne du Maurier. It had a special, other-worldly character. The house was big and solid, having a nucleus on to which was grafted a Victorian extension. Yet whenever I saw Harden, in its park-like setting above the water-meadows, I entertained the fanciful thought that, should I blink, the place would disappear.

The Rev Arthur Ingilby, of Harden, was a staunch member of the Church of England who sent a shock wave through the district when he married one of the Cadogans, who were Catholics. The original Ingilbys at Lawkland were adherents of the old faith. In times of religious intolerance, they held illicit services. If there was a hint of trouble in the form of official nosey-parkers, the hapless priest was bundled into a special hiding place.

Mrs Ingilby, tall and dark-haired, had a lively manner and an obsession with horses. She bought several white horses that were said to have belonged to Baroness Orcsy, the romantic novelist. Through his wife, Arthur Ingilby might have entered a wider social world. One of her friends was Lady Colin Campbell. The clergyman – a gentle man in every sense, was content with rural life. Their child, Christabel, grew up at a time when the family fortunes were being squandered. Mummy and Daddy had to sell Harden, along with its ghost, which/who was possibly associated with the priest's hiding place – the inconspicuous retreat in a corner of the room that became the kitchen.

Christabel took up residence in what had been the gardener's cottage. We saw her tall, thin, somewhat wobbly, wispy-haired and tweed-clad figure moving about the village. Sometimes there was a sad look on her face – a sort of Lady Anne Clifford look – as though in straitened times she was pondering on past glories. Then, when amused or interested, she would smile, a truly bright smile, as if her face had some inner source of light.

On the outbreak of war in 1939, Miss Ingilby tried to get into the Army by pretending she was some some twenty years younger. Her war service partly consisted of collecting war savings. She who had little spare cash told me of her amazement at how some of the Austwick folk had cash tucked away, not wholly trusting the banking system. She had visited an isolated farm and entered a kitchen that had whitewashed walls, a flagged floor (partly covered by pegged rugs) and simple furnishings, the centrepiece being a long table, with chairs at top and bottom and forms on either side.

The fireplace was one of the big, old-fashioned variety that demanded a weekly application of black-lead. On one side was a boiler and on the other an oven. The fuel was a mixture of firewood and dry peat. The mantlepiece had the usual Dales-type clutter of objects, flanked by pot dogs. Standing beside the opposite wall was a huge sideboard.

She explained why she was calling. "War savings? We've nivver heard of 'em." Miss Ingilby explained. "Well – we don't know if we can lay our hands on any cash just now." The tone was friendly. A search of the kitchen was undertaken. Money – a pound or two at a time – was plucked from obscure places, such as from under a pot dog, from a purple vase, from the corner of a drawer and from a rack that held several yellowing copies of the local newspaper. As they were found, the notes were placed on the table. Soon over £50 had accrued. Miss Ingilby's eyes were standing out like the proverbial chapel hat-pegs as she beheld this rapid accumulation of wealth.

When a local girl's beloved terrier was ill, someone told her that Miss Ingilby knew all about animals, so she went and asked her if she would look at him. She did and immediately threw her fur coat on the kitchen floor and knelt down beside the dog basket. Miss Ingilby pronounced that the dog had distemper and a vet should be summoned from Settle at the earliest.

Her life was frugal, as you might imagine. I recall an autumn evening. I called at her request to discuss playing a part in one of the Shakespearean productions she organised – an event in which half the villagers occupied the stage and the other half were spectators.

Christabel had her customary seat to one side of the fireplace, where wood hissed and spat. Looking at the finely-moulded face and the sad expression, I saw her come to life as she discussed *Macbeth*. It was my turn to look sad when she offered me the part of Banquo. I lacked the discipline to sit down and learn lines. Meanwhile, with the production little more than a gleam in her eyes, Miss Ingilby was keen to discuss the matter of hessian. She loved to say hessian. It would be used extensively in dressing the stage.

The cup of tea she offered me was not the type made by leaves bought from a Co-op. I was never quite sure of its origin, though basically preferred the Co-op blend. As she bustled in her little kitchen, I found I was under the unblinking stare of a Buddha, which stood on a low table. Local people who knew about it had the romantic idea it had belonged to Reginald, the most widely-known of the Farrers of Clapham because of his success as a plant-collector, author and rock-gardener.

Reggie had become a Buddhist and would dress in his eastern robes as he gave a show of his own slides. They [an unnamed source] said it was hoped that the Ingilbys and the Farrers would, through Cristabel and Reginald, be united in marriage. Instead, Reginald died ill, miserably alone, in a tent pitched on a rain-spattered ridge in upper Burma.

He was only forty years of age.

Macbeth was duly presented. As Banquo, I was attacked by an assassin in darkness on the apron stage, a precarious area, made up of several forms lightly tied together. The dagger held by Norman Burniston actually struck me, between two ribs, and the howl I uttered was heartfelt, startling the old ladies who were sitting on the front row of seats. Miss Ingilby would also utter an unShakespearean cry when part of the stage

collapsed, and she with it. There was a sigh when my "no frieze or buttress" became "cheese and futtress." *Macbeth* was enjoyable. And, such was the power of the words I was called upon to learn that when I next visited Austwick Hall for the whist results, I did not hear a tawny owl but "the fatal bellman that bidst the stern'st good-night."

Harden was sold to Dr Thomas Lovett, who came to North Craven from the Scottish Highlands via the glens of Antrim. He was irrepressible, living up to the family motto, which might be translated as "Never say die." When his wife Madeline gave birth to a daughter in 1905, she was very ill. Having recovered sufficiently to look round, she asked: "Where's the baby?" to be told: "Oh, she is out on the bay with her father." Young Dr Lovett, delighted at having become a father, had promptly taken the new baby for a sea cruise, with another man to do the rowing. It was said that such an introduction to the wider world was the reason why his daughter, as she grew up, did not suffer from mundane illnesses like the common cold. (I was told the story by that daughter, Sheila Lovett, who presided over Harden for many years).

Continued on page 65

Austwick in the pre-motoring age. *Above:* White-washed buildings round the main green. *Below:* The Green, looking towards Moughton.

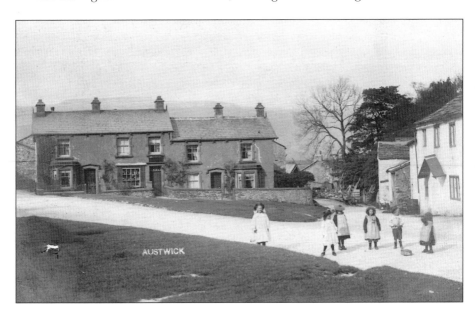

Two more pictures of Old Austwick. *Above:* A corner of the reception room at the Hall. *Below:* Jimmy Capstick, blacksmith, with his horse Jessie, used to convey passengers to Clapham railway junction.

In quieter times. *Above:* The Gamecock inn. Notice the mounting steps.
Below: George Truelove in his grocer's shop.

Yew Tree Cottage, a romantic name for our cottage in what the locals
called Methody Row. The official name was Spouts Croft.

Church Affairs

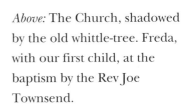

Above: The Church, shadowed by the old whittle-tree. Freda, with our first child, at the baptism by the Rev Joe Townsend.

Below: A Mothers' Union occasion. Left to right: Mesdames Richardson, Kirkbright and Townsend.

Left: Wooded Oxenber, photographed from Austwick Bridge.

Right: The author sitting on the trig point, Moughton Fell. Penyghent forms the backdrop. *Below:* Mothers' race, Sunday School picnic, Feizor, May 1958.

Above: Scene from a Shakespearean production at the parish hall. Left to right: Jack Swale, Kathleen Mattinson and Tom Guy.

Above and left: Frank Lambert and his horse Peggy using a side-delivery in one of Handby Ewbank's meadows. The horse was soon to be supplanted by a Ferguson tractor.

A Royal Day

Above: The village cross, decorated for the Coronation of Queen Elizabeth II (June 1953). The local Queen was Noreen Lambert.
Below: Austwick green, looking towards the Gamecock Inn.

The billiards room of the Ingilbys became the doctor's consulting room and laboratory. (He was forever conducting scientific experiments). A car bore him round the district. On a winter's day, summoned to a remote farm, he completed the journey on ski's. He took out tonsils at the patients' homes and was sometimes asked to travel to Leeds to administer anaesthetics in difficult operations.

Dr Lovett brough to Harden a patient from a remote farm who was about to give birth to a child, having sensed that it might be a difficult birth. He had noticed an absence of modern amenities such as running water and electricity. The child was born with a membrane over its head. The membrane had to be ruptured without delay. As he attended to the birth, the rest of the family backed him up with fresh linen and plenty of boiling water.

When Thomas Lovett's wife died in 1939, he gave Harden to his daughter Sheila. Her first memories of the place were when she called with her father when the Ingilbys were in residence. She heard about the ghost. "The family were forever looking for it." When, as a young lady, Sheila was returning to Harden from a dance and was wearing a shimmery sort of dress, she crept upstairs and, unknowingly, awakened her mother who, next morning, said she had actually seen the Harden ghost. Another day, their faithful old dog became aware of a "presence" and, with hackles rising and giving a steady growl, followed with his eyes the passage of some unseen object down the stairs, across the hall and out via the front door.

Sheila turned Harden into a guest house. She provided facilities for many parties of students undertaking field studies in the Austwick area. They admired oaken fittings that included pieces of a four-poster bed, the uprights serving as pillars and the headpiece adorning the fireplace.

None of them reported seeing the ghost.

8 - Church and Chapel

Architecturally, the church was as plain as they mak' 'em, having begun life as a chapel-of-ease to Clapham. There was no wealthy family to titivate it, as little Mrs Robinson used to say. The older generation of Austwick folk had an abhorance of "owt fancy" but did admire a stained glass window, installed to the glory of God and one of the Claphams of Austwick Hall. The organ had been good in its time but was now so temperamental that only one person – Captain Russell – knew where to kick it when a problem occurred.

When I first settled in Austwick, lodging with Mrs Bee, the vicar was the Rev J J Clack who, being virtually bald, had a well-scrubbed, ovoid appearance. He was a genial man who preached lively sermons – sometimes so lively that points were taken up by intellectually lively members of the congregation. Freda and I never fell out over religion. We simply went our separate religious ways – she to church, me to chapel. Our children were baptised by the Rev Joseph Townsend and became little Anglicans.

Holy Joe, as he was affectionately known to some, was a small, down-to-earth, woodbine-smoking man who was the proverbial spit-and-image of Arthur Askey and had the same restless energy as the radio celebrity. Joe got things done quickly. A farmer who was one of his wardens at Eldroth, and who liked to ponder over things, reading all the small print, said despairingly: "It's all reight as long as thou keeps t'cart on t'wheels." With Joe, you had to run to stand still.

I would call at the vicarage for a chat and to collect parish news for the papers. We would sit, on either side of a glowing fire, incinerating cigarettes by the yard. Joe would say: "I don't think there's anything to report this week." There rarely was. But by the time I left the house, I had two or three notes – gossipy notes, plucked out of the air. It was a time when I regularly filled half a column with Austwick chit-chat and when villagers were careful what was said to me. "He'll mak summat of it."

Donald Coggan, when Bishop of Bradford, loved to visit the district – to meet the farmfolk in their farmhouse settings and to preach at village churches. The story was told of another Bishop in another place who was about to take a service in a rural church when the Vicar gently reminded him that the congregation consisted of ordinary country folk, not intellectuals. After the service, the Vicar waylayed a farmer as he left the church and asked him what he thought of that morning's preacher. The reply was: "He's aw reet – but was he ivver eddicated?"

My favourite place of worship in the parish was at Eldroth. In July, 1630, Giles Moore of Eldroth and John Radcliffe of Keasden, and others, erected "a House at Eldroth for a Chapel for reading of prayer in, and for a school house, being about two or three miles distant from the Parish Church and having such waters between them and their Parish Church as many times are not passable neither on horseback or foot..." Indeed. The broad, squelchy valley between the two places was often standing in water and Austwick Moss, a resort of naturalists, had affinities with the Everglades.

Generations of local children were grateful for the basic education provided by Eldroth School and when the school closed the old building, with its one-bell tower, lived on as a church. When I gave a slide show here, the place was packed and the ladies provided refreshments. They had to bring every drop of water for brewing tea and afterwards go outside to rinse the crockery in bowls.

Austwick Methodist Church (more commonly known as t'Chapel) was opened in 1901, succeeding an older place of worship. As far back as 1806 "five members made up this little society." By 1815, there were thirteen members – "yan more than t'disciples" – who met under the leadership of William Baynes. The records of the Manor Court, held yearly at the Cock Inn, Austwick, included a note relating to the opening of the first chapel. Twelve jurymen found William Baynes, tenant in trust by an indenture dated 24 May 1824 from Richard Jackson Baynes, "of a certain Piece of Ground in Austwick containing a length of 27 feet and in width 25 feet or thereabouts, where about a Methodist Preaching House has lately been erected, being within and parcel of this Manor, under the yearly ancient rent of *one penny*, with other dues and services."

The chapel had no architectural pretensions. It was every child's idea of a building, with a door and two flanking windows. The escutcheon over the door bore the date 1823. Inside was a pulpit, a harmonium and a gallery, stepped up so that all might see the preacher. He in turn could not help but notice the large clock attached to the front of the gallery. There was bound to be some crusty old Methodist sitting near and ready to cough loudly if the service exceeded the allotted span of one hour.

I like to think of Mr Baynes as I think of many another old-time Methodist – a forthright, down-to-earth chap who called a spade a shovel and having his own colourful interpretation of the Bible. I can imagine him giving vivid word pictures that might not be literally correct but got over the point he desired to make. "T'king summoned Jehu – he was that mad charioteer – and told him to drive to Jezreel so he could give Jezebel a bit of his mind. And when he saw her, in her fancy place, he said: 'Chuck her down'. And they chucked her down." In its early days, rural Methodism owed much to men like Mr Baynes.

A convert stood up at a Class Meeting and said: "Some folk think I'm cracked." The Class Leader promptly said: "Let us pray. O Lord, crack a few more; there's plenty of work for 'em to do in thy Kingdom here on earth." Older folk had "heard it said" that some mischief-makers had dramatically interrupted one of the chapel services by setting a cartwheel rolling down the road from the green. It burst open the chapel door. If this had happened when Mr Baynes was preaching, he would doubtless "mak summat of it."

In comparison, the new Austwick chapel shouted to be noticed, having a commanding position overlooking the green and a flaring red-tile roof. The 1950s saw the last great flourish of Methodist fervour, when hymn-singers rattled the windows, the prayers made even the flowers on the communion table weep and the sermons were as homely as a fireside chat.

For a mid-week gathering, stalwarts crowded an adjacent vestry, where a harmonium (described as "an ill wind that nobody blows any good") was to be found, a yard or two from a fireplace. When I conducted one of the mid-week meetings, the only place available was in front of the fire. I should have taken as a theme the Fiery Furnace. The lusty singing and the wheezy voice of the harmonium combined to create a din, especially when someone chose a hymn set to the *Londonderry Air*, with its high-pitched note, and the retired quarryman, so delighted he managed to "hit" it, hung on for a second or two with an effect like that of a factory hooter.

The Sunday School was the big open space beneath the chapel where scholars met on Sundays and were given an insight into the religious way of life by Misses Byles and Wade who, if truth were known, had been brought up in the Congregational Church. Children from the farms joined those of the village. One farm lad, shown a picture of Moses, remarked with derision: "He's a cobbed [strange] 'un."

Little Mrs Robinson, a temperance fanatic, met with members of her Young Abstainers' group. One hoped that children of between five and seven would be able to keep off the hard stuff, which was more than Mrs Robinson's husband had been able to do. One of her total abstinence friends at Keasden repeatedly asked a small boy if he could write his name. Each time he said he had not yet started school. "Tell me when you start school and learn to write your name." He did. "Show me how you do it." She proferred a large sheet of paper and he laboriously wrote

69

down his name. Years later, he discovered he had "Signed the Pledge," vowing he would never drink intoxicating liquor.

Chapel folk loved a social, especially one incorporating a Jacob Join tea, for which food was contributed by those taking part, being put in a common pool. It's your stomach 'at 'ods your back up. The fare was plain and wholesome. Here were sandwiches and scones, Eccles cakes and jam tarts, sponge cakes and fruit cake so rich it clagged the stomach. A variant on the Jacob's Join theme was the Faith Tea, another case where food was pooled. Tea was "mashed" in a kitchen area that was high-tech – in the Victorian sense.

The chapel itself was used only for the two Sunday services. The pulpit had the grand proportions of the bridge of a small coaster and, painted on the wall behind, was a religious text. To the right of the pulpit stood an organ which, during the time of my membership, was electrified – not "electrocuted," as the minister of the time, Eric Roberts, patiently explained to an old lady who had the wrong idea.

The pews of varnished wood were of uncompromising hardness. Above the door through which the preacher and steward passed on their way from the vestry, at the start of a service, was a clock with a plastic frame – a clock which reminded the preacher, if no one else, of the remorseless passage of time and, hopefully, when he might bring his homily to a close with the word almost everyone looked forward to hearing, namely "Amen.'

In the 1950s, a retired couple kept an authoritarian grip on Austwick chapel – and also on the minister. They didn't want "any fancy ideas." The minister must "stick to t'Bible." There were giants in those days. He had the craggy face of an Old Testament prophet and such a powerful physique that, when singing, he could hold his hymn book ("with tunes") at arm's length without wavering. His voice "rattled t'rafters." She, well-built, tall and brooking no nonsense from anyone, presided over the organ.

Her assistant, Mr Batty, pumped air into the venerable instrument, sitting on a little form at one side and operating a lever connected with the bellows. He did this uncomplainingly. If, during a prayer, when heads were bowed and, theoretically, eyes were closed, I happened to sneak a view of the other worshippers and an eye eventually lit on Mr Batty, he would give me a broad wink. At a funeral service when the hearse with its precious load arrived half an hour late, the organist – this time one of the family – filled in the time by playing Handel's *Largo* incessantly. This musical item fell to the bottom of any Austwick list of popular tunes.

A chapel service on Sunday afternoon was a trial for all concerned, especially in summer when, having had a good lunch, and sitting in patches of sunlight, at least one worshipper fought to keep awake. When his wife was "off colour" and stayed at home, he was instructed to give a full report on what had been said and done at the service. He dosed off. Being normally taciturn, he had little to say when the time came to report to his wife. "Who was the preacher?" "Mr Smith." "What did he preach about?" "Sin." "What did he say about Sin?" The by-now-weary husband, who in truth had heard little of the sermon, sighed and replied: "He was agin it."

The most demonstrative worshipper at Austwick Methodist Chapel was the retired quarryman. He had been brought up in the days when preachers stoked up fears and nurtured hopes; they had a no-holds-barred approach to religion. Our quarryman friend latched on to every word and responded vocally to every well-made point.

I equated the quarryman's well-moulded face, his bushy moustache and thatch of grey hair with everyone's idea of a Swiss clock-maker. He was a sensitive soul who during his working life had been tormented by swearing and, occasionally, blaspheming quarrymen on the lorry taking them to work in Ribblesdale. He opted to travel by bike, which he did in all weathers. One day, it is said, he had a strong head wind and prayed that the wind might change direction. His prayer was answered. He had a head-wind on the way home.

He went with a party of fellow Christians to the week-long Keswick Convention. On his return, I asked him about the experience. He had attended every prayer meeting and every service. What effect had the Convention had on him? "My head was a bit thick by Wednesday."

This man was one of the last of the old-style emotional Methodists - the type of worshipper, once common in rural areas, who responded to well-made points in prayer or sermon with a heartfelt "Amen" or "Hallelujah." One local preacher, who was classified as "modern" and whose words were treated with the utmost suspicion, in case he led the Flock from the way of righteousness, induced the old man to give an anguished cry of "No, Lord! No Lord!" If the hymn was "one of t'old 'uns," he was certain to start singing the last verse for a second time, taking the rest of the congregation with him.

Chapel hymns were of the lusty type, with choruses. The prayers were long and repetitive, with no pause in the verbal flow to give God a chance to answer back. One of the villagers called us God-botherers. Sermons tended to be long rambling affairs. One old-timer was fond of testifying, bearing witness to his conversion and to the effect that his new-found experience was having on his daily life.

He equated his conversion with that of St Paul, blinded by a bright light on the road to Damascus. He would begin: "Friends, I were crossing top pasture wi' a calf bucket on me arm when I saw this bright light in t'sky. It fair dazzled me. I wor that capped I nearly dropped t'calf bucket."

There must have been times when God just had to laugh.

9 - Haytime

In summer, the smell of new-mown hay pervaded the village. The most aromatic species of grass was called Yorkshire fog, a name that bemused strangers, especially when a farmer was offering some fog-grass for sale. At Austwick, the floriferous meadows lying between the three peaks of Norber, Moughton and Oxenber were mown, dried by wind and sun, and stored as winter fodder for the stock.

The local farmers were "keyed up" at the approach of haytime. I made a point not to engage any of them in conversation but to agree with everything that was said. Otherwise I might find my head "snapped off." In poor weather, a farmer was thoroughly depressed, yet when the clouds parted and the sun glowed like a blow-torch, he became a super-man, managing on little more than four hours sleep a night for ten days – or maybe even a fortnight.

The usual labour force at a farm was insufficient to cope with hay-time. Extra men were hired. Farmers living near the village made do with "night men." Most of the hay was being led from field to barn from late afternoon until the evening, which appealed to men with daytime jobs. Fred Price was one of those who worked for Handby Ewbank year after year.

T'auld chaps told me of a specialist labour force, consisting of battal-ions of Irishmen, who arrived to help out on the farms of northern England. The men, who came mainly from County Mayo, in the far west of Ireland, were known as "July Barbers." An Irishman was usually hired for a month, at a figure that included food, lodgings and – quite often – a barrel of ale. They were rarely well paid and never, never over-paid.

Austwick farmers had hired their men at Bentham. The farmer's wife decreed where the Irishmen should sleep. Most of them were accommo-dated in the farmhouse, but some were provided with a loft or hut in

the area of the outbuildings. Such accommodation was sparsely furnished. When an Irishman arrived at a farm, his few possessions were
kept in an attache case and carrier bag. On Saturday night, he was working in his old togs. On Sunday morning, when a calm descended on the
Dales, for no self-respecting family worked on the Lord's Day, the
Irishmen emerged like butterflies, each wearing a white shirt, blue suit,
brown shoes or boots. They set off to walk to the nearest Catholic
Church to attend Mass.

Afterwards, they resorted to the nearest inn. Up Keasden way, the
Irishmen were late returning to the farm and one of them yelled
upstairs – for the family was in bed – asking if a friend of his he had met
might stay the night and perhaps be found a job of work. "Aye, lad," said
the farmer. "Bed him down somewhere and at breakfast-time we'll see
what we've got." It proved to be the champion whisky-distiller of western
Ireland. He was asked to make a list of his requirements and was
excused haytime duties. He must concentrate on distilling. The "still" he
fashioned from a few simple objects was subsequently in a loft at the
farm for many years.

Having promised to help with haytime, I was duly summoned to fields
that had so many flowers, they were in glorious technicolour. Peggy, a
stolid, unflappable horse, trundled round with a two-wheeled cart that
was normally used for muck-spreading but which now had shelvings [a
light wooden framework that fitted tightly on to the cart to increase its
capacity for carrying hay]. Each load weighed no more than five hun-
dredweights, so the shuttle service between field and barn was incessant.

Haytime was hard on men and horses. The inexperienced men, such
as me, quickly developed "water blisters" on the hands. The horses,
especially the youngsters, became sore about the shoulders through pro-
fuse sweating. Sore horses were bathed in salt and water. One farmer
filled some of his wife's old stockings with hay and used them as a pad
between the shoulders and the harness. The horse called Peggy

belonged to Frank Lambert. During that first haytime, he heaped praise upon her. She was a "grand 'oss." (Next year, she was missing from the hayfield. When I asked Frank where she was, he replied, succinctly: "Meat!")

Those were the days when the meadows teemed with life. There were rabbits galore. Curlews, now with the care of half-grown young, were demented when the field gates were lifted from their hinges and the haytimers with their simple machines arrived in fields that had been peaceful for many weeks. An old hedgehog grunted to itself as it made its evening rounds of the dyke-bottoms where, with the coming of dew in the evening, big fat slugs were moving.

Bountiful Nature could also be irritating in every sense of the word. With the coming of dusk, midges flew in tawny clouds. Swat one of the minute tormentors – and a thousand midges would arrive for the funeral. Sometimes I found what appeared to be a small black grape adhering to my leg; it was a sheep-tick, bloated with blood – my blood! I had been told not a flick it off or the head would remain under my skin and a septic leg could result. The best way of dealing with a sheep-tick was to dab it with 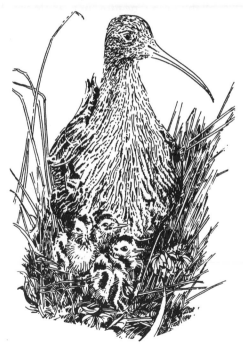 the hot end of a cigarette and risk third-degree burns. A man who used whisky as a tincture was told by the doctor: "Are you trying to drown it?"

Frank, an early acquaintance in the hayfield, was fond of his old Dales expressions like: "Thee kem yon cart down." When I got a second opinion, I gathered that he wanted me to take a rake and remove from the load on the cart any loose material that might drop of during the long haul to the barn. That word "kem" meant to comb, according to a dialect dictionary published early last century.

It was Frank who told me about the days when the meadows were mown by scythe – by a large, straight-shafted scythe that had an enormous blade. He had heard that four men, working as a team, mowed an acre in the best part of two hours. At the head of Austwick was a farm called Dear Bought. The story was told of a man who wagered he could mow the home meadow in a single day. He did – then dropped dead!

With their long-handled scythes, the Irishmen had "broken out" the edges of a meadow, allowing unimpeded access to the single horse mowing machine. Now the meadows were being mown by an appliance attached to a Ferguson tractor. Frank gave me a reminder of days of yore – a strickle, which was a four-sided piece of wood that was attached to the shaft of an old-fashioned scythe and contributed to its balance. The sides of the strickle were covered with an abrasive material and it was used to sharpen the blade. Frank remembered when he was sent to a moorland tarn to collect fine, hard sand – scythe-sand. The strickle was pitted with holes, greased down using bacon fat or the like, and then powdered with sand, the grains becoming lodged in the holes.

At haytime, every farmer prayed for a long, settled spell of weather. He rapped the barometer with the gusto of a woodpecker at the nesting tree. He was alert to weather signs. He listened to every forecast on t'wireless. It was bad, said the farmers, if the hills appeared to be close at hand. It was good if cattle were grazing on the hilltops with light showing between their bodies and t'ground. A glishy [gleaming} sun in the early morning presaged a day that would break down with rain by noon.

Holding wooden rakes, we worked rhythmically along the swathes and turned them. When the hay had been "strawed" and then rowed-up, it was transferred to the cart by a man holding a long fork. He advanced up a row, fork before him, pushing against the row of hay until a considerable heap was formed. Then, binding the heap with deft movements of his fork, he lifted it high and placed it on the edge of the cart, where a stacker awaited it. The man with the fork was careful to turn the tines so that his friend on the cart would not be punctured.

The hay was stacked in a prescribed order and to a height of several rounds; it would be removed in the reverse order when the barn was reached. A small forkful of hay – of the type I used to deliver when first I did the work – was described witheringly as "a bird's nest." When a load was ready to be transported, a little ritual was enacted. Stout ropes that were attached to the back of the cart were tossed over the load. Now each in turn was pulled by several men so that it was tight before being tied to the front of the cart. One man directed the operations; he was usually standing on the cart. His voice rang out clearly: "Pull, pull, pull, pull – and tie!"

In chancy weather it was necessary to secure the hay against rain and this was done by making small, well-packed heaps, the tops of which would turn the water. The basic heap was known as a "foot cock" and two placed together, on on the other, was a "hub." A much larger heap (a "pike") secured the hay for a longer period. Some farmers piked most of the hay in the fields and led the hay from pike to barn.

The old farmers were fussy about leaving a field clean. They did not want to see a wisp of hay. My very first job in a hayfield was "raking out dyke-bottoms." I graduated to using a Red Rover, a large metallic rake that was pulled by hand across the open field. Sometimes I found a tuft of bright green grass, which had been missed by the machines and had not been converted into hay. I would inquire from Frank what should become of it. He would yell back: "Purrit in wi' t'hay; it'll help it to sweat!" And so it did. Hay, taken in rather damp, soon gave the barn the humidity of a Turkish bath. I visited a farmer in his "longhouse" type of farm, in which a stout wall separated his living quarters from the barn, under a single capacious roof. The hay in the barn was sweating so vigorously the wallpaper in the living room had become damp and was beginning to peel off.

Cooking meals was a prelude to haytime. The farmer's wife knew that the men would be "famished." Haytime suppers had been memorable. During the war years, Mrs Whitfield had carried out into the meadow a selection of pies and custards and great urns of tea.

The main meals were taken indoors. Tea was usually served in the open. The food contained in baskets and the tea in metal cans. At other times, the men refreshed themselves with cold drinks left in the field. On non-Methodist farms there was ginger beer in stone bottles. Nettle beer was made in large quantities; it was cheap. Some farmers bought *Mason's Extract,* a herbal preparation, and "let it down" before bottling it for use. It was powerful stuff. Every year, corks left some of the bottles with the velocity of bullets. Elderflower champagne, another cheap preparation, was a refreshing drink.

Thence to the farm, first to wash off the dirt and hayseeds. The farmer's wife provided bowls of hot water, towels and soap for the purpose. The last meal of the day was usually memorable, taken after dark.

10 - Over the Counter

Scene: A crowded butcher's shop, adjacent to a slaughter house and to a croft in which prospective joints and steaks are still on the hoof. Norman, the butcher, also retails homely comments, some pertinent and others just impertinent. He talks as he chops or saws lumps of meat or adroitly twists into neat shape long strings of sausages, in the preparation of which he uses herb-flavoured meat and no bread. Not even in the darkest days of the Second World War had Norman resorted to mixing meat with bread to make it go further.

Middle-aged Lady Customer: "I want a nice bit o' meat and not so much bone. I don't mind bone now and again – but not every time!" For once, the Austwick butcher is subdued.

Norman, a jovial man wearing the traditional blue and white striped smock, usually met every eventuality with a laugh, in marked contrast with Jack, butcher, who having been to the local inn, would moodily complete throwing himself off the bridge into a deep pool "and have done wi' it." He never did.

I saw more of Jack and his wife, passing their little shop during the working day as I headed for Clapham post office. Jack's wife decided to augment the family income by serving fish and chips on certain days. I became her first and almost the last customer. She knew I contributed to the *Craven Herald* and asked me if I could send off a note about her fish and chip business. I did. The note was published.

When next I saw her, she looked doleful, reporting: "I'm giving up my fish and chip business." I thought the publicity might have stimulated trade. It did. Among the readers was the sanitary inspector, who visited her premises and said that before she resumed cooking she had to conform to the regulations, which included tiling part of her kitchen, having special facilities for hand-washing and wearing a special smock.

I digress. Let us return to consider Norman, the Austwick butcher. In the days when the horse was master of the dusty road, his father had wise-cracked his way through the long days. While mincing beef, in a shop well-filled with customers, he addressed a lady who had moved from Hartlepool to be housekeeper to a rich old farmer living on t'tops. Said the butcher, cheekily: "I suppose you're sleeping with him." She put him in his place by remarking: "What's t'point of making two beds when one'll do?"

Shortly afterwards, the farmer drove through the village. Everyone noticed that painted on the back of the trap were his initials, coupled with those of the housekeeper. As he explained later: "Farm lad put it on. Afore I could get a sec [sack] to it, paint had dried." He may have liked the idea of his name being associated with that of the house-keeper, who was what the old 'uns of Austwick called "a comely woman."

The butcher took an apprentice – a lad fresh from school – and on the first morning he handed the boy a whittle, which was a small knife, and said: "Catch yon sheep – an' cut its throat." The lad recoiled. "I couldn't do that," he said. "Well," said the butcher, "just catch the sheep." The lad did so, after much effort. He pursued it round the croft half a dozen times before he cornered it. Even the sheep was getting weary. Dragging the luckless animal to the butcher, the lad remarked: "Where's that bloody knife?"

It was a marriage of opposites. Norman's wife was a tidy, refined lady who kept an immaculate house, never dropped an aitch and once actually had a lodger. He was a professional young man with a passion for Rugby. At the butcher's house, he received gargantuan meals and, despite his daily exercise and the Saturday rough-and-tumble of the Rugby field, his weight increased at an alarming rate.

Harry Lord, our local postmaster, was also something of a weather forecaster when sheets of new stamps were delivered. "It's going to rain," he might say. "Look how that sheet of stamps is curling." He delivered local letters himself. Postmen ventured into the outback settlements of Feizor and Eldroth on foot or bike. Bibby's had the nearby greengrocer's shop, from which a mobile shop went forth.

A village shop was a cal 'oil [gossiping place]. When an occasional visitor mentioned that her neighbour had died, she was asked when this happened. "Let's see; if she'd lived till tomorrow, she'd 'ev bin dead a fortneet." Another, inquiring about a friend's husband was told: "He's just had another injection." "By Heck," said the inquirer, invoking an old north-country god, "he must be like a pin cushion by now."

A weary rambler, who had slumped on the village green, gave a shilling to one of a group of lads. He asked him to get a pork pie from the shop, which was advertising them at 4d each. The rambler added "and get one for yourself." Minutes later, when the lad returned, his mouth was full of pie. He handed over 8d change and said: "They'd only one pie left." An abrasive woman who inquired about candles, firelighters and paraffin, and was assured that each was in stock, said: "Wash your hands – and cut me half a pound of ham."

An astonishing range of goods was carried by the Austwick shops. (The expression Jack-o'-the-Pinch was used for goods a person had forgotten to buy elsewhere, as in Settle on market day). Austwick offered "tinned stuff" and bottled sweets, butter and bacon, cauliflowers and cough cures, in glorious disarray. As in the butcher's shop, there was much lively banter – and also some serious talk, such as about taties. A gardener who confessed to planting King Edwards was told by a fellow gardener: "Ah reckons nowt to Majestics. They sup up all t'gravy."

Clare Pierson, of Harrogate, a good friend of *The Dalesman*, sent a poem about a Dales corner shop:

We have some somewhere, luv, I know
I had 'em in my hand, by gow.
Eh, Florrie, hasta seen them nails?
Them half-inch 'uns we sell from t'scales?

Tha what? In't bath? Then cum on down,
Ah've got shop full. Put on thy gown.
Ah'll see to thee, lad – what's thi pleasure?
A yard of beadin'. That's good measure.

Now lass, an' how's thi mam today?
Ah'm reet put out to hear that – nay.
I thowt that she were pullin' round.
Come on, Florrie – he wants a pound.

And Winnie here wants one o' them
Pink pan scrubs, they were in a tray.
Tha's put 'em on't top shelf, by heck,
Tha's bahn to hev me brek mi neck!

The doyen of Austwick shopkeepers was George Truelove – tall, lean as a greyhound, grizzle grey as a badger and somewhat gangling, as indeed he might be, having a wooden leg. No one dare ask him about it but he could hardly keep it secret, for Mr Truelove was in the church choir. When he processed with other choristers down the central aisle of the church, everyone heard the dull thud of the artificial limb.

George had an ancient Austin car on which he bestowed much love as well as polish. To see him driving through the village, heading for Clapham station, was an impressive sight. A rough wooden notice high up on an outbuilding advertised "motor carriage for hire." Closer inspection revealed that at some dim and distant time the message had been "horse and carriage for hire." The first words only had been modified. Why waste good money on paint?

It was the classic corner shop. You couldn't miss seeing it. When George, under-employed indoors, was in the garden, pretending to tie up rose trees, his eyes willed you to enter the shop, which had the obligatory jangling bell above the door. George made an almost operatic appearance. In less than a minute after the door bell had ceased to ring, he appeared through a door from the house. That door was at a much higher level than the floor of the shop, so he looked down on you from a great height. I did not know Mrs Truelove but was told that she was "round and had very red cheeks and was only marginally less alarming than her lord and master."

I heard from a lady of a childhood memory concerning Mrs Truelove. "I went to the shop with a puppy-dog. As I stood and waited for her to wrap up the groceries I'd been sent to get, I saw to my horror that tiny Jock was practising his new-found skill of lifting his leg without toppling over. Unfortunately, he was practising it against a sack of something by the door. I knew this would not go down very well with Mrs Truelove, so managed to stand protectively in front of him while the wrapping and paying was going on. Unfortunately, just as we were leaving, a telltale trickle began to make its way across the floorboards. Suddenly there was a shriek from up high of *'your dog's peed on my oatmeal'*.

"I'd no idea what was the right thing to do in such circumstances. I remember vaguely thinking there must be some etiquette that adults would know about, so I just stood, frozen. This must have infuriated her because she advanced on me exclaiming: 'How would you feel if I came and peed on *your* oatmeal?' The very idea so terrified me that I just scooped up the wretched pup and fled..."

When asked for sweets or small commodities of this and that, George deftly twisted a sheet of paper into a cone. A poacher was keen to master this technique. He had heard from a friend of one way of catching pheasants, which was to have such paper cones smeared with treacle and holding small quantities of corn. These were left where pheasants fed; they were soon visited by the birds which blundered around with them on their heads.

George, the oldest shopkeeper in the district, had presided over his careworn wooden counter for some 50 years, since the days when butter, lard and sugar were delivered to him in bulk and he weighed them out. The shop then was flavoured with many scents, some of them unknown in Arcady. When I first knew him, in the days when nearly everything had become prepacked, the shelves were stacked with an impressive collection of painted containers for spices and teas, also (empty) cartons to give the effect of a range of goods. Now the dominant smell was of disinfectant. The potato crisps I bought were flaccid.

George remembered when butter and eggs came straight from the farms. Selling them to the grocer provided a farmer's wife with "ready money" or she might barter the farm produce for groceries. Before the First World War, butter produced at Crummack Farm, a few miles from the shop, was retailed at ninepence a pound and you might buy a score of eggs for between tenpence and a shilling. Rabbits were sold for a shilling a couple and cock chickens at 1s.3d (sometimes 1s.4d) a pound. Home-cured bacon was available at fourpence-halfpenny a pound. The village grocer "bought owt they had and selled them owt they wanted."

If he had sold the shop, he would have been "fast for something to do," so he laboured on, fretful at any loss of trade. When a new vicar patronised another shop, George left the choir in a huff and became even more of a recluse. When he died, the rows of ornate containers for dry goods that were worth a small fortune were tossed on to the tip at Helwith Bridge, to be picked up by a delighted (and disbelieving) antique dealer from Settle.

Travelling shops were in vogue. A mobile grocery was operated by John Alan Foster, from Bentham – a lile man, with a brisk manner. He would ask: "Is there anything else?" Then run through a list of available groceries at 400 words a minute. I was tempted to ask him to repeat it. Once a month, we saw "the man who brings the pots and pans." George Hugill came from Burnley but he was of good Swaledale stock. The family moved to Lancashire when the lead-mines closed. George was a well-made chap with a ruddy complexion, described by our neighbour Mrs Handby as "like the rising sun."

To George, our house was a stopping-off place, where he had a seat by the fire, a cup of good strong tea ("hot as hell and black as t'fire-back"), sandwich or scone. He yarned about his hardware career with a horse and cart; in snowtime, the balls of snow that formed under the horse's hooves had to be kicked off periodically. Now George had a large van painted chocolate-brown, with the words "Over Sixty Years Reputation" painted on each side. I sometimes inquired what sort of reputation he was claiming.

There had been an earlier van. It perished in flames one autumn evening as he drove home from Feizor. George had not discovered the fire until he reached Gisburn. He was told later that flames and smoke were pouring from the back of the van as he passed through Settle. All he had when he arrived back at home was the fire extinguisher.

On his rounds, George had met drovers with their cattle. One of them was Owd Mick, "the bull-walloper," who had a reputation for being able to drink twelve pints of ale to twelve strokes of the clock. He had suffered a throat injury in the First World War and could no longer gulp. Mick's ale-supping could not possibly match his reputation but those who heard about it were anxious to test it out, so he had plenty of free beer. George told me he met the oatcake man, whose laden basket was neatly balanced on his head. As he walked down the lanes, he swung his arms and occasionally rang a bell.

One snowtime, as he turned into the lane for Feizor, he asked a road-man about his prospects of getting to the little hamlet. "You'll get there all reight." There was a way but it was not quite wide enough for the van and the sides scraped the snow, producing a sound like that of a circular saw. The doors could not have been opened if he had wished to escape; the only exit would have been through the windscreen. "I think that was the beginning of my hair turning grey," he said with a chuckle.

As the years went by, George's stock went through a considerable change. The demand for "dolly sticks," to be used on washing day, declined. Oak dolly tubs were replaced by the galvanised type. Black lead, no longer used for fireplaces, was still handy for piano keys and as a lubricant for wood. When rural folk ironed their clothes with charcoal irons, George had a big trade in charcoal.

For one glorious winter, Don Mills brought a fish-and-chip shop into the village. If there was a light breeze, the tang of vinegar seemed to permeate every corner of every house. To eat fish and chips in the frosty outdoors was a pleasurable sensation until the fat cooled into thick grease as it seeped between the fingers.

11 - Herd-letting

On a Saturday evening in February, farmers with interests in Moughton, Oxenber and Long Scar (Ingleborough) gathered in the "supper room" of the parish hall for what was called the herd-letting. The name had nothing to do with cows, herd being short for shepherd. A dozen men, their faces scrubbed, not merely washed, and their tweedy clothes smelling faintly of moth-balls, arranged their seats around an open fire and prepared for two hours of talk and five minutes of business.

With much outcropping of rock on the local hills, an acre was of little significance from the point of view of grazing stock. So the hills were "stinted" for grazing purposes. Each farm had been allotted a certain number of stints, a stint – also known as a gait – representing the grazing for one sheep. Moughton had 568 stints, there were 579 on Long Scar and a mere 120 on Oxenber Pasture. Four sheep gaits equalled one cow and eight were needed to keep one horse.

Grazing took place between specific dates. Thus the hills carried as many sheep as the vegetation could stand, which was based on long experience, for the secretary kept an ancient calf-bound minute book. The first entries were in graceful copperplate; the latest in blotchy ballpoint.

John Chapman, who frequently teased me, a townie, by lapsing into dialect, turned and said: "It's nippy toneet. I reckon t'auld yows'll be bleeatin' for a bit o' fodder." The men at the herd-letting were sheep men to the core. Since their earliest days, they had followed a routine established in Norse times, a thousand and more years ago. One of them had told me: "Some folk say I think more of my sheep than I do of t'missis. I suppose I do. If owt happened to me, she'd be able to look after herself. But who'd tak care of t'sheep?"

His year began in November with tupping time. His grandfather had spent a month salving his sheep, shedding the wool in rows and applying a mixture of tar and grease to the bared skin with his finger. Harry Holden had told me of the Black Hand Gang. Those who salved sheep absorbed some of the tar and it took a while to clear. Harry had a relative who was married at salving time. "When he stood at t'altar with his wife, his hands were as black as t'Ace o' Spades."

In April, when winter grudgingly relaxed its grip on the hills, it was lambing time. The year rolled on to clipping, then spaining, when yows and their lambs were separated and t'farmfolk could hardly sleep for a night or two because of sheep bawling for each other. And afore a chap knew where it was, it was tupping time again...

Billy Fell, who was a little self-conscious at being chairman/secretary/treasurer/committee and owt else that was going, took the calf bound minute book from its brown paper wrapping and opened it at the page on which last year's decisions had been recorded. If he had turned back to the first page, he would have seen the magic date, 1814, which – as farmer once observed – was the year before all that fuss at Waterloo. He might also have noticed that the herd-letting official at that time had written in glorious copperplate. Billy and his immediate predecessors were inclined to scribble, using a ballpoint pen.

The air clouded with an acrid cloud of smoke from the darker forms of tobacco, which were being incinerated in pipes. The non-smokers were sucking mints – always mints. I had a theory it was to offset the bitter-sweetness of the cow muck they dealt with every working day.

"I suppose we'd better start," said the chairman, right on time.

"What's thee hurry?"

"Nay..."

"Aye, let's get it ower wi'."

No shepherds had tendered for the job of looking after the sheep on the stinted commons. The farmers were reconciled to doing the work without help. The minute book held details of the men who had shepherded the local hills. Harry Ballard had been the last to serve on Long Scar. In 1947, he was paid 1s.11d a gait. T J Ward, the last official shepherd on Moughton, had done the work in 1945 and was paid ls.9d a gait. C Constantine received ls.10d a gait for shepherding on Oxenber in 1943.

The meeting went on to consider a farmer who had been overstocking the pastures. He did not usually attend the herd-letting. A chap who lived nearest to the overstocked land gave a resumè of recent events. "When I first browt matter up, yon hill was fair wick wi sheep. Tha could hardly see t'grund between 'em." Such an exaggeration was justified where such an important matter was involved.

"We've telled 'im about it."

"Aye – and for a time he seemed to have takken heed. Yesterday, I saw t'farm lad driving aboot sixty sheep off t'hill. That number was just about reight. I said to him: 'Them sheep look in good condition.' He said: 'You should hev sin all them sheep I browt down yesterday'."

I managed to stifle a laugh. To the farmers, it was no laughing matter. Few things were. There were grave looks all round and talk of legal action.

Billy Fell entered details in the calfbound minute book, shut it with a snap, and talk drifted to other matters – like farming, farming and farming.

12 - Parish Hall

The Supper Room was used for meetings of the Women's Institute. First there was a rendering of *Jerusalem*, to piano accompaniment. I recall how upset one of the members was when she reported that the Labour Party conference had used "the W I song" at the end of their conference. And with what merriment it was related that at one Institute, the minutes had contained a note to the effect that "new copies of *Jerusalem* have been ordered because our words are dirty."

Each meeting started with a consideration of business matters. The pile of outstanding correspondence went down with painful slowness, like the sheaf of notes used by a long-winded preacher at the chapel. "And finally..." usually meant that the business session was half way through. If anything womanly was being discussed, there were broad smiles in the direction of the solitary male, the speaker, who was sitting near the door.

The person who introduced the speaker usually managed to make it amusing, though the merriment was not always intentional. "I am deputising for our President, who is on holiday. How we all wish we were with her." Harry Scott swore that at one Institute the presiding lady said: "At our last meeting, I agreed to get a celebrated wit as the speaker for this month. I couldn't get a wit, so I have brought two half-wits."

My least favourite event in the Parish Hall was a whist drive, particularly the Christmas whist drive. Everyone except myself played to win. I regarded the event as a bit of fun. At the start of a game, one farmer from off t'tops, wearing his best-setting off suit, complete with moth balls in the pockets, held out a hand which looked like as big as a dinner-plate, and I was invited to cut the cards, not on the table but on the vacant part of his hand.

Not having that much interest in whist, I sometimes revoked. This led to baleful looks and even anguished cries. They rose to a wail if the event happened to be the Christmas whist drive, with good prizes for the successful players. The "Ingleton lot," who toured the pre-Christmas whist drives throughout the district, were disgruntled if they did not return with at least one turkey or goose.

Once there was a shock. The goose was alive and, judging by its violent movements in a sack, very well. For once there was no desperate effort by the ladies to get the premier prize. They would be content with the box of chocolates or bottle of summat or other. The winner did not live in the village. One of our thousand channels of information reported that she had become attached to the goose, had given it a name, fed it with household scraps – and couldn't bear to see it killed.

The liveliest events at the parish hall were dances. The dancing tradition was kept up by middle-aged and elderly folk and the music was unashamedly sentimental. Dancing provided escapism and exercise for those who had not yet been imprinted by television and who still enjoyed setting out to enjoy themselves locally.

I loosened up my limbs by attending country dance sessions in what was grandly known as "the ballroom" at The Traddock, initially under the stern gaze of Miss L M Douglas, who in the 1920s had toured the

91

Dales and persuaded rheumaticky old gentlemen and ladies to tell about and – if possible – to demonstrate the dances they knew when young. She had recorded music, words and dance instructions in two booklets. The dances included *Square Eight, Huntsman's Chorus, Kendal Ghyll, Brass Nuts* and *Meeting Six*.

Freda and I had picked up the steps of more modern dances at farmers' dances in Skipton Town Hall, where skill needs the support of stamina and an acceptance of pain as heavy shoes or even boots crunched on our feet in progressive dances. I once sweated out a nasty chill by incessant dancing in a well-packed room. Normally, the *Gay Gordons* was like a cavalry charge. When *The Lancers* were held, and middle-aged farmers showed us how to do them, they swung their partners so vigorously they were lifted off their feet.

I o n I c u s

On dance night, the parish hall was its own spartan self. Those attending were the types who were unimpressed by flashing lights and electronic wizardry. Music for the first Austwick dance that Freda and I attended was provided by two players – a middle-aged lady pianist and her "young" man who had a supporting roll on the drums. The stage at the parish hall looked not much bigger than a window ledge. On it stood a piano which, as they say, had known better days. It had also known drier days, for the pianist was inclined to put a cup of tea on the top and occasionally it slithered into the works.

As a chain smoker, she rested cigarettes on the keys so that in due course most of the outliers were all-black. Sometimes she kept a cigarette in her mouth and played – with her finger-tips, as far as I could see – squinting as she was enveloped in an acrid cloud of tobacco smoke. Her young man played with that rigid adherence to beat that makes me want to look round the back, expecting to see a large clockwork key turning slowly.

Latterly, we had the Beresfords, members of an old Dales family of music-makers, to give wings to our feet. The music of piano accordion and drums blended well and at the correct tempo. Harry Cockerill, who was related to the Beresfords, was a somewhat legendary accordion-player who imparted the old Dales flavour to the dances he attended.

Harry, who like most of the Beresfords was self-taught, remarked: "I don't know a note of music... My type of dance music is the same as it's ever been. I've played same tunes ever since I started – and they still dance to 'em.'""

The old tunes were the best. Some had the flavour of Music Hall and others were the popular songs of the First World War. Among the Top of the Dales Pops were *I Do Like to be Beside the Seaside.* We responded to the invitation to *Let's all Go down the Strand* or found our voices as the band played *Down at the Old Bull and Bush.*

Dancers came from distant places, undeterred by a few flakes of snow. An old couple related to me, quite calmly, how they had driven home to Dent on a snowy road that had shrunk to the width of a council plough. Austwick dances were slow to "warm up." There was a chattering among old friends – just a few friends at first. The main hall tended to become crowded at about nine o' clock. It was then that supper was served.

For some reason, there was always a progressive dance, known as *The Friendly Waltz* just before the time for feasting. As I progressed, from one lady to another, there were times when I bruised my fingers on corsets as hard as armour and when the other hand became damp from clasping hands, some of which were knarled with age, some hardened with ceaseless work, some soft and some distinctly sweaty. I contrived as the strains of the music began to float into nothingness to dry my hands on the back of the dress of the lady who was my partner at the time.

There was a drum-roll, a clash of cymbals, the floor cleared, the sliding door of the supper room was opened and into the room came helpers with trestle tables holding plates of food. It was hardly a banquet. Each received a plate holding two sandwiches, a bun and a slice of cake. Tea was served from an urn and delivered through a hatch, though at one memorable Young Farmers' dance it was poured from a ladle that had been dipped in a bucket. Sometimes I think I must have imagined seeing a bucket containing hot tea being taken round the room.

No one wasted much time drinking and eating. They had come to dance. An old chap told me: "If I didn't git up an' dance, I'd lock up wi' arthritis."

Once I was jerked from a bath-tub reverie by a reminder of an evening slide-show appointment I had forgotten. There I was, lying in a soapy swell, at peace with the world, when the telephone rang. Seconds later, Freda appeared, somewhat excited, reminding me I was to give a slide show. The people had gathered. The lecturer was half submerged, and about to reach out to the hot water tap to raise the water temperature for another languid spell of bathing after a busy day.

I arrived in the hall twenty minutes late, still steaming, and with some trepidation went through the old routine of lifting a floorboard and fumbling in the dusty gloom for an electrical socket into which I could place the plug attached to my projector. I should have been wearing rubber gloves. That evening, my talk began with the words: "A funny thing happened to me on the way to this meeting…"

The parish hall was the venue of the flower show – the event which, as I mentioned, was called the Lords' Day because members of the Lord family claimed most of the trophies. Thinking of my own miserable efforts at gardening, I was astonished to see turnips as big as footballs and marrows like monster balloons.

I became secretary in curious circumstances. An emissary from the organising committee arrived on the doorstep and reported on a recent meeting at which I was invited to take over as secretary. Touched by the gesture, I agreed to do the work. The minute book was handed over to him by the emissary, who promptly fled.

Relief? No – possible embarrassment. There had been three meetings of the committee when a new secretary was needed. The first two people to be asked had turned down the job.

13 - The School

An old picture of Austwick school showed a close-packed group of desks and children, neatly dressed, arms folded, backs as straight as exclamation marks. One of the old-time headmasters, W L Carradice, had qualified as a trained certificated teacher in 1884. When asked if he had any trouble controlling a large class briefly replied: "No." He'd come from Kettlewell, in Wharfedale.

Boys were not breeched [clad in trousers] until they were five years old and ready for school. Prior to this they had been dressed like girls. A handkerchief was safety-pinned to jersey or pinafore so the teacher could quickly attend to a dripping nose. Most children wore clogs. There was a tattoo on the roadway as knots of children – even quite small children – walked from scattered hamlets and farms, with a few sandwiches for lunch and the promise of summat hot for tea.

Attendances were vital to the teacher who had no fixed salary; he was paid by the Board of Education in the form of a capitation grant on average attendance. "Passing the Standards" was also important; these were set by the Board and concerned what became popularly known as the Three R's – reading, 'riting and 'rithmatic, plus religion. It was vital he "kept in" with the local vicar.

Object lessons were part of the system. At Kettlewell, if a boy had killed a rabbit on his way to school, there would be a lesson on the rabbit. If the headmaster, who was keen on rural pursuits, caught a trout, he could organise a lesson dealing with fish. The school had an outdoor garden, made up of road-sweepings, and an indoor garden. Two laburnums flourished happily until two small girls ate laburnum seeds and had to be taken home for emetics. There followed a lesson on "cutting down trees."

The walls of an old-time classroom were adorned by pictures representing the Seasons, with happy children, bouncing lambs and contented-looking cattle and sheep. There was also a map of the world, with the land masses mostly tinted red, forming part of the British Empire. In days of yore, a dominant sound was the squeak of pencil against slate. Most other sounds from the children were punishable.

Children were taught to be seen and not heard.

The school was divided into two classes, with windows set high, to discourage children from looking out on the world. Information was disseminated through repetition, punctuated by the swish of the cane. In the case of spelling, by dint of learning three or four new words a day a child's vocabulary gradually extended. In an art class, a farmer's son was having trouble painting the sky. A helpful master put in some fluffy white clouds. The lad from the wet and windy dalehead said: "Sir – where I come from, t'clouds is mucky."

The old folk who told me about Austwick School had left at the earliest age, which was thirteen, then raised to fourteen. Some left early on compassionate grounds, a parent being ill. Yet most of them could read fluently and write legibly. Sloppy writing had been frowned upon. Left-handed writers had their "defect" corrected and entered the world as right-handers. Respect for authority was taken for granted.

By the time we lived in Austwick, education was more varied and discipline was maintained without brutality towards young folk. The 1944 Education Act had removed the Great Deterrent, the cane, which had been a compulsion to learning, yet in village schools such as Austwick the teachers would not "stand for any nonsense." Happily for them, most of the children were from farms, where young people had any naughtiness knocked out of them and in their young days had absorbed the work ethic. Some were performing simple jobs not long after they had graduated from wearing nappies.

Austwick School still had high-set windows, blotting out views of the world, but bright colours abounded in the classrooms. Clogs had been succeeded by boots or shoes. Slates had been disposed of, though the blackboard was still a vital part of the educational process. The squeak of pencil on slate had gone, but the squeak of chalk on blackboard continued. And the headteacher, while engaged in blackboard work, still had eyes at the back of her head.

Miss Macdonald was a good headmistress. The children stood in awe of her. What she said was remembered – or else. She could punish a child by a quick change of voice or by eyes that fixed the wrong-doer like the eyes of a stoat transfixing a rabbit. She lived in a detached house at Town Head and was friendly with the nearest farming family. She occasionally appeared at Mrs Bee's and was dragooned into playing one of the protracted card games.

During the long summer break, Miss Macdonald, as she was universally known, was one of the helpers when George Whitfield and his family were making hay. I also helped. School was never mentioned. Her particular fondness was for the Red Rover, a large metal rake, with long curving fangs, which she hauled up and down the meadows that had been freshly cleared but were strewn with wisps of hay that must not be wasted.

If frustrations had built up in the classroom, Miss Macdonald was able to release the nervous tension by a three mile walk up and down in the same field. As we forked hay on to a tractor-drawn trailer, she was a solitary figure in the landscape, endlessly moving up and down the field with the huge rake slurring behind her.

When our children, David and Janet, began school, they were

enveloped in the arms and loving care of Connie Wilson who, though uncertificated, achieved striking results. For a few weeks, mothers who inquired from their offspring what they had been doing were told: "Weeding, whiting and kayoning" [reading, writing and crayoning]. Connie was endlessly patient and ensured that before children moved up to Miss Macdonald's class they were well on the way to being able to read and write. Some had achieved the skill of joining up their letters.

Soon the children were able to assist their parents in reading a pre-bed story. (They certainly knew the moment a weary father tried to skip a page or two in his haste to get a bairn into bed). An appetite for the written word was quick to develop. In their spare time, boys entered into the delights of comics printed in lurid colours. One child was fascinated by the Meccano catalogue, with its colourful pictures and terse descriptions of the model vehicles on offer.

Rural kids soon developed a realistic approach to life. When, during a Scripture lesson, the teacher read to them the Parable of the Lost Sheep, it was natural for her to ask why, if there were ninety-nine sheep in the fold, the shepherd should be keen to get the missing animal. A farmer's son put up his hand, then said: "Appen [perhaps] it were t'tup." During another scripture lesson, the teacher asked: "Who is the Good Shepherd?" A boy replied: "Me dad. He's just lambed fifty – and not lost one."

The children contributed to a nature table. The changing seasons were represented by varying displays of objects and flowering plants. The most touching moment of the year at this and every other Dales school was the annual Nativity play, which we as parents dutifully attended. The time-honoured story was told interspersed with carols. Mary selected her favourite doll to represent the Christ Child. Joseph was invariably a bluff farm lad.

One year, the innkeeper who had no room to offer the Holy Family was heard saying to a friend: "I blames Joseph. He should have booked."

14 - Field Club

Every bit of damp ground was "tewit grund," being colonised by lap-wings. They heralded the spring. Within a short pram-pushing distance of the house, we heard the cock birds' plaintive cries as they nose-dived, flutteringly, and pulled out of the dive when we were convinced they were about to crash. Will Pritch and others were still "partial" to a break-fast of plovers' eggs. They took them knowing the birds would lay more clutches and that, anyway, the first eggs were likely to be frosted. Nesting stood a better chance a little later in the year.

Every meadow had its curlews, which stalked with heads down, long curved bills delicately picking up morsels of food in meadows which were becoming green and sappy and abounded with insect life. To some villagers, it was the curlew, not the tewit or the cuckoo, that proclaimed springtime. "Thou can cod [deceive] a tewit but t'auld curlew 'ods back till there's summat good to sing about." (We had not reached the fully mechanical stage of farming, when many half-grown curlews would end their lives in bales of hay).

The high ground held a scattering of golden plover, whose melan-cholic call had one reaching for a handkerchief. I loved to climb Norber when one or two pairs of "goldies" were in residence, their crowns and mantles peppered with gold. A white stripe separated the upper parts from the sooty-black under the plump body.

Some aspects of natural history were studied by naturalists and round-ly condemned by farmers and gamekeepers. The carrion crow, which was Enemy Number One because it plucked the eyes from ailing lambs and made a general nuisance of itself, was ruthlessly persecuted. Some birds were shot. Others were enticed into small cages by the plaintive calls of a captive crow and the nests of these big handsome birds dressed in feathers of undertaker-black were dislodged using a long rod known as a "crow poker."

The gamekeeper needed all his wits to discourage crows, foxes, stoats, weasels and poachers.

Austwick had long had a Field Club, which catered for those who liked an evening saunter in the warmer months and lectures of various kinds in winter. The highlight of the summer programme was "Down the Beck for Birds," led by Dennis Byles, a retired water engineer, or Willie Mattinson, formally William Kinsey Mattinson, who was small and spare, as were his wife, his sister and his family.

He was the nearest Austwick got to a tycoon, presiding over an agricultural supply business. Willie Matt loved the outdoors and when not inhaling fresh air was tainting his lungs with pipe tobacco. For a time in his young days he focussed his attention on cave exploration, finding remains of early man and early beasts in limestone caves at Cave Ha' and having Kinsey Cave was named after him. He was an authority on the Amazon, though he had never been within a few thousands miles of it. Infused with enthusiasm for the subject, he contrived to read everything that was published in book form about the mighty Amazon, so that if you had set him in a small boat at the mouth of the river, he would have been able to find his way along its navigable reaches with full knowledge of its topography and wild life, especially piranha, the river's celebrated carnivorous fish.

His daughter, Kathleen, a nephew (and me) were among the small party of Field Club members who set off one summer morning to visit Gaping Gill, which – this being a Bank Holiday – had a gantry in place to provide potholers and visitors with a bosun's chair descent of 340 ft into the underworld. Willie Mattinson was interested in our excursion. As a small boy, he had been in the party who gathered at GG in 1895 and saw a lile Frenchman, Martel, make the first-ever descent and, just as important, the return.

Martel had done so with rope and rope ladder. He had a lantern fastened on his arm and attached to the wooden bar on which he sat was a waterproof packet containing candles, magnesium and a flask of rum.

When we visited Gaping Gill, potholers were clad in boiler-suits, with ex-miner helmets to protect their heads. The bosun's chair descent was available to anyone who wished to take an easy way to the underworld. It cost nothing to descend. A charge of ten shillings was made for the return journey.

The bosun's chair was guided into the enormous shaft by a strong cable. The only other sound was the hiss of water falling over twice the height of Niagara on to shingly floor. The sensation of being like a spider dangling from the roof of a cathedral ended when the brakes were applied on the winch high above and the chair stopped a foot or so from the ground. Hands freed me from the harness, a potholer in the queue of those wishing to ascend was fastened in. I watched him – a dark blob – rising into the spray from the waterfall, which was in part the beck, diverted from the lip of the shaft and finding another course underground.

I turned to greet the member of the Bradford Pothole Club who was on duty. Kathleen Mattinson was to be the next person to descend. I told the potholer that she was the daughter of a man who had watched Martel descend. He grunted. There followed Willie Matt's nephew. I said to the potholer: "This is the nephew of the man who watched Martel descend." The potholer grunted again before remarking: "You'll soon be telling me that bloody Martel's on his way down."

One Field Club expedition was to Oxenber at dusk to listen for the curious song of the nightjar, a sound that Willie Mattinson remembered from his young years. Alas, the nightjars were Absent Without Leave. Chris Cheetham, our most distinguished naturalist, looked like an overgrown schoolboy, habitually wearing short pants, his pockets being full of clutter. Chris's old cottage overlooked the main green. When he was at home, he was oblivious to general views, having his head in books or one eye pressed against a microscope, his window on a mini-world of wondrous forms and colour. Chris exulted over such things as plant tissue and the legs of crane flies.

He had arrived in Austwick during the 1930s as a refugee from the textile industry. He craved for freedom and expressed his new status as a countrygoer by not shaving nor wearing long trousers. There was a concession in winter when his long shorts were overlapped by long stockings to protect him against wind and weather as he cycled down the lanes or scrambled up the scars.

Chris led some of the Field Club outings, which took place on Saturdays. Once, the interested members cycled to Lawkland, where the walk was due to begin. Mrs Bee had not mastered the art of cycling so Chris took her on the back of his tandem. Here she sat, behatted and very upright – an awesome sight.

When describing a bird, a plant or an insect he spoke with slow deliberation, so he would not be misunderstood. The first time I went botanising with Chris, I ranged over a field looking for splashes of red, yellow or blue which to me indicated flowers. Turning, I saw him kneeling a few feet inside the gate of a field. When I sheepishly returned, he not only pointed out a dozen or so common plants in a patch of ground the size of a pocket handkerchief but plucked a few leaves of this and that and invited me to taste them. I discovered that salad burnet tasted of cucumber. I was less keen to try the various species of fungi that Chris nibbled in the field or took back home for his breakfast. He said there were relatively few poisonous species. The art was in identifying and ignoring them.

Chris, a long-serving secretary of the Yorkshire Naturalists' Union, carried his seventy-nine years lightly. He did not cloud my mind with technical phrases or Latin names and, when he had to use a Latin name, he apologised beforehand, adding: "I don't think it has an English name." His own name, as Cheethami, was bestowed on a species of daddy-longlegs he had described for the first time.

Chris was a cyclist. He estimated that his bikes had carried him about the north-country for half a million miles. "Cycling is the only proper way of moving about the countryside," said the man who, when he was over seventy and his mother over ninety, they were to be seen travelling through the district on a tandem.

He kept unsociable hours, careful not to reveal the presence of a rarity to those who might pluck it. When most people were in that pre-awakening period of "driftin' and dreamin'" in their beds, Chris would be half way up Ingleborough or Penyghent. He knew where Jacob's Ladder grew. He was familiar with the location of rare ferns and once, showing me the holly fern, on limestone, he partly covered it up so that it would continue to thrive but would not be easily seen by collectors. Chris knew Austwick Moss like the living room of his cottage. The walls that lace the district were interesting to him because of the moss and lichen that clung to the old stones.

Chris had an accident while cycling from Austwick to a Yorkshire Naturalists' Union meeting at Scarborough. He broke a leg. Heads were shaken sadly by people who did not think he would ride a cycle again. In a surprisingly quick time he was back in the saddle. When he was provided with a metal hip joint to replace one that was arthritic, he had to arrange walks so that in hilly country the least weight was placed on the patched-up hip. Once, as we left Oxenber, Chris turned to me and said: "They made a good job of that joint. But it gets a bit stiff. It's a pity they didn't leave a hole so that I could oil it."

One of the Field Club lectures featured Tot Lord and his account of the "bone caves" of the Langcliffe and Settle areas. The bones included the remains of beasts that roamed the area well before Tot-time. The oldest were dated to about 120,000 years ago. Tot Lord, who had married one of Charles Lord's lasses at Austwick chapel, was light-fingered when holding a gun. Theoretically, he was a greengrocer, but in fact he did almost everything else, including buying and selling property and furniture, stripping down cars, selling parts and then putting the torch to the rest to recover the solder.

At other times, he would go wildfowling, mainly around the Ribble flood-plain south of Settle. Here he shot what he called a white goose, though it was almost certainly a whooper swan. He took it home for his wife to cook. There was so much to eat that long before the skeleton had been laid bare Tot's family was sick of the taste. Tot shot duck and geese, some of which were old enough for their flesh to bend a dinner fork.

Richard Fawcett, alias Rabbity Dick, who lived at Clapham but knew the Austwick district well, called in to see me at *The Dalesman*. Dick, like the wild creatures on which he preyed, kept unsocial hours, mainly dawn and dusk, for he was by calling a railway signalman. His accounts of poaching were later given permanence in book form. Dick was the sort of chap who poached game and disposed of vermin but, at another time, could become tearful as he described a fledgling bird or a particularly fine sunset he had seen. He was one of those sharp-eyed countrymen who could detect a crouching woodcock on its nest of oak leaves by the sparkle in the bird's eye.

A remarkable story involved Dick and a family of hedgehogs. At Clapham, his home abutted the old railway line, a section of which formed part of his garden. Bantams nested in the garden and Dick was perturbed when eggs began to disappear. Then he found the culprit – a hedgehog. Feeling kind-hearted, he put the hedgehog in his car and drove to the other side of Newby Moor (which, where it is crossed by the A65, is known to visitors as Clapham Common). He released the hedgehog and drove back home.

Not long afterwards, he heard a faint whimpering in the shrubbery and found a nest containing young hedgehogs. He had just disposed of – mother! Dick went to Settle, bought a fountain pen filler and some nourishing liquid and returned to gather up the young hedgehogs to feed them. This was necessary every two hours, day and night, until the hedgehogs were beginning to thrive. Then, a day or two later, he found a hedgehog in the garden. It was presumably the hedgehog he had left a mile or so away. She had negotiated the cattle grid at the gateway without falling in. She completed the rearing of her family after all.

Rabbity Dick was said to have used the railway for unorthodox jobs, such as sending a live badger in a crate from Arkholme station, where he was temporarily based, and (reputedly at Clapham) to have rid the district of some unwanted goats by dropping them, one by one, from a railway bridge into passing goods wagons. There was consternation further down the railway system when the stowaways were detected.

Will Pritch, who was in the front rank of Austwick characters, waged war against "them craws," by which he meant rooks that nested in t'Whittle Tree, beside the church. I would see him early in the day as he stood by the bus shelter, looking anywhere but towards the little rookery (known to one village lad as a "croakery"). When he felt to be alone, he nipped into the bus shelter, picked up his gun and discharged it towards the tree. I do not recall any of the rooks being killed but there was a fair smattering of pellet holes in the tree.

Will, who did not join the Field Club, having "summat better to do" than "gallivant about t'place looking for birds," did not let the topic of "them craws" fade and in winter, when all self-respecting rooks were roosting elsewhere, he would stand up at the parish meeting, regardless of the topic being discussed, and demand: "What about them craws?" Each spring, Sally Pritchard, his characterful wife, led a party of youngsters to see the raven's nest on Moughton. Every child called her Auntie. She was indeed related to most of them. Children of all ages responded to Sally's warm personality. And she was the only aunt in the village who organised field excursions, trudging across fields, fording becks and (if need be) climbing walls.

I cannot recall the raven-hunting expedition ever came within viewing distance of the raven's nest. One of the children would fall and badly graze a knee. Or young legs would weary. They would eat whatever provisions they had and return to the village. Each reported at home that he/she had had another glorious day.

Austwick had one or two notable naturalists who abominated groups and worked alone. Charles Lord built up an enormous collection of ferns and could talk interestingly about them. To walk through his garden was like being in a miniature tropical forest for all that was in sight were green fronds. He also had a passion for religion. When he said: "What do you think of Matthew 21?" it was time to flee, for it was the prelude to a diatribe on the sorry state of the world.

15 - Farmfolk

Some of the farms had intriguing names – Dear Bought, Jop Ridding, Gayclops, also Israel and – Rome! Some were situated on sweet limestone; others lay just across the geological fault, where the outcropping rock in the sour landscape was gritstone. When a summer visitor asked an Austwick chap about the Craven Fault, the answer he got was: "The folk are far too abrupt."

An intrusion of flagstones about Moughton Fell had its uses as flooring and for making water cisterns, boskins [divisions in shippons] and benks [shelves in outbuildings]. Where water bubbled out of the ground near the head of Crummackdale, it had exposed a smooth rock known as "whetstone," once in demand for fettlin' the blades of knives and scythes.

Most of the local farms were small by modern standards. It was said of one place: "There's a bit o' good land but there's not much of it." The farmsteads that intrigued me most were those named Israel – one a cottage, the other a farm that, at the very edge of human memory, were occupied by the Wildmans and the Garths. I entertained the idea of visiting one or t'other, asking for a glass of milk and then writing an article for *The Dalesman* headed: SPENT THRUPPENCE IN ISRAEL.

My first view of the cluster of buildings that abutted the moor was after walking on the hill where, in snuff-dry conditions, I had kicked up heather pollen with every footfall until my boots were uniformly grey. Remote Israel had about it something of the mystique of a desert fort. Here, in times long past, was the home of Jack Wildman, the gamekeeper, and Molly, his wife. She had been a Jackson from nearby Kettlesbeck. The area teemed with red grouse. In a bad winter Jack would awake to find a few birds perched on the yard wall. Once, so near was the moor, he found a covey of grouse clustered on his doorstep.

Every February, a farmers' ball was held at the Wildman home at Israel. "There wasn't much room," I was told by Norman Swinglehurst. "The dancers were as rank as sardines in a tin." The dance went on until daybreak. Some people danced, some sang and some played cards. Thomas Airton played his violin for the dancing. "He played too fast and nearly killed those dancers who were daft enough to try and keep up with him." Old John Garth had a white beard. He also had the customary large family, named Ellen, John, Tom, Bob and Willie. John, a stay-at-home, wore long fustian trousers that he split up the sides from the bottom; it made it easier for him to don them!

Farm folk were generally un-romantic types, like the plain, matter-of-fact Norsemen who had settled hereabouts over a thousand years ago. A man who courted a lady for so long she got "fed up" of him, received a letter from her in which she said he must either "go right" or not at all. The way he was going, he was keeping other men away! She sharpened him up. He "went right" – and married her!

Families were much smaller than of yore, when they were apt to run out of ideas for names for their offspring.

An insight into t'auld days was given to me, not long after I had moved into the district, by Mr Nowell, of Stockdale Farm, Feizor. I found him sunbathing, fully-clad. He wore a flannel shirt, minus collar; waistcoat and coarse-woven trousers. As he sat in the sunshine of a perfect summer's day, his head was cast in shadow by a Panama hat. He had donned it despite the protestations of his neighbour that by doing so he'd "brek t'weather."

Mr Nowell was one of those who mentioned Old John (John Wilman) who was a sage in Feizor and, on nights when clouds swept over the fells and hid the moon, stared upwards and remarked "t'village lantern's gone out." This was also the case in the 1950s. When the moon hid its face, the farm folk used storm lamps as they moved about, had oil lamps in house and shippon and kept a reserve of candles "in case of emergency." An average household was using between six and eight gallons of paraffin a month.

At Austwick, we looked through the windows of Yew Tree Cottage and saw farm folk passing in Land Rover or on tractor. At muck-spreading time, the sickly-sweet small of farmyard manure – locally known as muck – pervaded our homes as the pungent stuff was being transported from barn-midden to revive some jaded meadows. In late summer, we enjoyed the smell of new-mown hay as Handby drove a load along the main street on his way from meadows at Harden Bridge to a barn at Town Head.

Austwick itself had a sprinkling of farming families. The Chapmans overlooked the Green and the Whitfields were at Hobbs Gate. There were Robinsons near Austwick Bridge and Morphets at Town End. The Ewbanks lived at Yore House and had their farm at Town Head.

The Austwick farmers did not need to resort to t'wireless for weather forecasts which, in any case, scarcely applied to a district where the landscape and grand undulations and at times clouds drifted about trying to find their way out of the little dales. A man like George Whitfield would confidently set out to walk up Crummack Lane, en route for Beck Head or the Sheep Dip, or whatever, having prophesied exactly what the weather would do by noon and by evening. He was usually right – however unlikely it seemed in the early morning.

A scattering of retired farmers and farm men throughout the village ensured that agricultural matters featured in most local conversations. One of the ex-farm men upset his tidy wife at spring-cleaning time by referring to it as "mucking out." Some of the still-active farmers were bow-legged wi' brass and could afford to employ a man to help out with the mucky jobs. The farm men were being paid about £3 a week for their efforts.

The workforce once included occasional helpers. They turned up to give a hand when sheep had to be salved. "They didn't come from anywhere; they just roamed t'country, getting a bit of a job here and there." One, called William Atkinson, nicknamed Ditheram, received, for his efforts, "a pair of fustian trousers and a new shirt." Alf Leek was, for some curious reason, known as Opplefrog. William Thornborough, who specialised in mole-catching, was naturally known as Mowdy.

A "lile chap" from Low Bentham helped out on some of the farms. His best efforts were at a place where the farmer, exploiting a weakness in the labourer, was continually singing his praises. At milking time at night, the farmer would walk backwards and forwards, up and down the shippon, saying: "Me lad, Billy, me lad – you're a reight good milker." Billy, who was "a bit simple," nearly killed himself to live up to its reputation. There were three outbarns at this farm. The farmer watched for him, coming back from attending to young stock in the first barn, shouted: "Well done, Billy," and Billy would run to the next barn. Mostly, by the 1950s, the work-weary "brothers to the ox" were content to make ends meet, though there were enough farm men to keep up the local population and – pending the arrival of lots of "new settlers" in the village – help to fill the church and chapel pews and provide sufficient children to maintain the village school.

One or two farmers managed to live off their losses. They had pride. And pride costs nowt. Frank, who had been reared at Slated House, distinguished between Farmers and Others. At some stage in a conversation, he would say: "He was a farmer." I felt like standing to attention and saluting. Farm children were soon dedicating their lives to "addling brass" and they had a bonus in some years when a bountiful nature filled the fields with mushrooms and providence brought a stream of cars along the A65, which lay half a mile or so from the village street. For several weeks, freckle-faced lads from the farms dedicated their spare time to selling mushrooms, to such an extent that in one of his sermons Joe Townsend referred to the strip of road verge between Cross Streets Inn and Harden Bridge as the Golden Mile.

When I visited an old farmhouse in one of the outlying hamlets, I might have been walking back into the nineteenth century. The farmer and his wife, wearing clogs, clattered about on flagstones hewn from a quarry at Helwith Bridge. When newly-washed, the flags had an appealing shade of grey-blue. Water for the house fell as good clean rain on the capacious roof and was directed by guttering and downspouts into an outdoor cistern made of the aforementioned flagstones, the several slabs being held together by red or white lead, plus iron bracing made at the local smithy. In a limestone area, where water was "hard," such "soft" water as flowed from the cistern was used mainly for washing purposes, leading to economies in soap.

Inside the kitchen, in the days of do-it-yourself plumbing, there was but a single tap, from which gushed spring water, plus freshwater shrimps, algae and goodness knows what else. The fireplace was of the huge iron variety that demanded a weekly application of black lead. On either side of the fireplace were boiler (the only major source of hot water) and oven. A clothes-rack dangling from the ceiling could be lowered or raised using pulleys. At one farm I saw what appeared to be a row of wash-leathers hanging up to dry. It was oatcake, a staple food, best eaten when plastered with "a bit o' June butter."

Farmhouse fare was not always as appetising as presenters on television imply. It might be plain and stodgy. The first requirement of a farm man on being hired was food. He would ask someone locally: "Is it a good bait shop?" Breakfast included home-cured bacon, sometimes so fatty it dribbled from the edges of the mouth. Dinner was once a matter of taties and something else. It might be dumplings. A farm lad whose plate was overladen with taties looked hard and long and then observed: "I think t'spuds have etten t'dumplings."

The farmer's wife used to brew beer for haytime. Sometimes it was "dish-watter stuff." Rabbits paid the rent, so to speak, and also featured on many a meal. At one farm, where some town lads were staying for a few days, rabbit was served at every meal, so that on the last day, when a beaming farmer said: "I suppose you'll all be ready for your rabbit pie," one despairing lad said: "What we want is *a bloody ferret.*"

Change was under way. The competitions organised at the Women's Institute brought the kitchen skills of most farmer's wives to the stage where they might win prizes with their scones, pasties and cakes.

When the Brown family were at Crummack Farm, water was drawn from a pump. A visitor from the village was to remember being offered a drink from it. "A glass was held under the pump and this great stream of water came gushing out, catching all the colours of the rainbow. The taste was unlike any water I'd ever known. A few years later, I was back there and the farmer's wife told me she had a tap in the kitchen now. I said I supposed that must make it easier. "Yes," she said hesitantly, "but it's fiddlesome. When I'm in a hurry, I go out to the pump."

16 - Moorland Ways

It was Bill Wallbank who told me about a most unusual sheep-washing. The washing took place about a fortnight before clipping-time. The farmers repaired to a dub that had been used for generations. This was dammed up, using perhaps an old door and lots of sods.

A man stood waist deep in water and sheep were thrown at him, one animal at a time. He would "riffle" the wool. The water removed muck, grit and the last traces of salve that had been applied the previous November. This went into the beck, stupifying the trout, but as the trout acquired a tarry taste no one felt inclined to eat them.

Bill's tale was about the time his father went into the yard early one washing-day and discovered his favourite dog had gone. Neighbours arrived. They too had lost their dogs. It was suggested that the animals might have gone to the moor-edge dub, which had been prepared ready for the sheep. The dogs were there. They had rounded up the sheep. As Bill said: "One dog was in t'watter, weshing sheep. Another dog was chucking sheep in." I asked him what his father's dog was doing. "Oh," said Bill, "it was going round wi' t'whisky bottle."

This was a rare occasion. Farmers were not inclined towards telling fanciful tales. Most of them found farming far too serious a subject for flippancy. One Sunday afternoon, when I was taking a service at a moor-side chapel, I began a somewhat imaginative tale for the benefit of the children. An old chap shouted from a back pew: "We want none o' thee fairy tales here!"

In spring, the moor came to life with the return of the upland waders – with curlew, redshank and golden plover. The grouse, imprisoned in their calluna desert, were already in their territories, the cock birds having shouted at each other with their coarse voices, *kowa, kowa*, which sounded to humankind as though they were calling *go back, go back*. In summer, the heather bloom was strong enough to empurple the under-bellies of passing clouds. In autumn, gunshot raked the coveys of grouse. In winter, the survivors and a few auld crows kept some semblance of life on high ground by their flight and calls.

No one knew more about the heathery uplands than Jack Wildman, of Israel – he who worked as a gamekeeper for Aldrick Watkins of Austwick and was paid £30 a year for his pains. He suffered badly from leg pains and died aged 66 years. The under-keeper, Jack Wallbank, received £15 a year. He lived at the farm known as Ing Close and was a versatile chap, touring the district, as far as Malham Moor, to castrate horses. "He was nearly a vet and made his own green salve." Jack also went into Bowland, pig-killing. When a pig had been slain and hung up, the men carded all night. Next morning, Jack was on hand to cut up the pig into the required pieces.

I found a tract of moorland, lagged with peat, thatched with ling, a refreshing change from the austere limestone hills.

The moors began less than two miles away. So I was assured by Mrs Bee, who said that her bees collected nectar from the moors and this was their operational range. Mrs Bee's heather honey was dark and viscid. Some of her friends gave the bees a helping hand by moving hives to the moor edge in late summer, when the bonnie heather bloomed and gave the impression that a giant had laid a purple carpet across the hills.

The moors led over to Bowland. From some of the highspots I saw the gleam of sunlight on Stocks Reservoir and was reminded of the time I took a party of lads from Austwick to visit an island gullery, courtesy of Mr Steel, the representative of the Water Board in these parts. Those were the days when I had the old Ford, and when every car trip was an adventure, with no guarantee that the engine would keep running.

Boys whose eyes were tuned to finding bird nests in obscure places landed from a motor launch to see the ground covered with nests. The gulls that swirled noisily in the air resembled a blizzard that refused to settle. There is no more raucous, nerve-shattering sound than the alarm calls of black-headed gulls. We moved slowly around the island and on our return to the boat there was evidence of boyish humour in the way that eggs from several nests had been piled high on the nest of a hapless pair of birds.

Back in the car, I drove over the Knotts. There was an occasional mysterious series of "cracking" sounds. I pondered on which feature of the car would collapse next. Eventually, I localised the cracking sound. It came from the back seat where four small boys were sitting with rueful looks on their faces and yellow yolk seeping from beneath their jackets. They had put gull eggs down their shirts so they would be undetected before they arrived back home.

The moors were maintained for the benefit of grouse and sheep and so that from the Glorious Twelfth the shooters had plenty of avian targets. Whenever I entered the moors, I did so cautiously, expecting at any moment to be rebuked for trespassing. I came across the old shooting huts, where the sportsmen and beaters gathered, never the twain to meet, for each hut had two rooms – one for the gentry and one for the paid servants. A roofless hut made this social division plain for all to see. The gentry area was overgrown with grass and the other section by nettles and thistles.

When the season for culling grouse arrived, Aldrick Watkins invited his friends to join him. Meanwhile, he arranged for provisions to be sent to the moor from the Gamecock Inn. One year, the bread had been missed out and the beaters were faced with "a lump of beef." Normally there would have been sandwiches. Then someone suggested they could still make sandwiches by "having two pieces o' lean beef wi' some fat in t'middle."

I had a special liking for Bowland Knotts, where the sad, two-note whistle of the golden plover was heard. Along the ridge was the ALE rock, which did not imply there were licensed premises. The carved letters marked the place where the parishes of Austwick, Lawkland and Easington met.

The farms of Eldroth were scattered along the moor edge and, at Keasden, formed a string of farms, the land hard-won from the moor. Lying over the whole landscape was a futuristic pattern of drystone walls, the changes of stone indicating something of the underlying geology, for no one would carry a stone further than was necessary and most stones were picked up or quarried near at hand.

Looking at a stretch of wall that had been gapped revealed there were two walls in one, held together with through-stones, tapering with height and being well supplied with capstone. Harry Holden, who used words sparingly, did point out the difference between the funny-shaped gritstone rocks that, once in place, endured so that a wall would stand even though it was beginning to lean. A limestone wall, composed of small rounded stones, collapsed the moment it began to lean. Harry who, you may recall, was our neighbour in Austwick, was a waller who gave a new wall a sure foundation, who crossed all the joints and was generous with the number of through-stones he used and capped a wall with stones that would endure.

The hill farmers talked for ever more about sheep. One farmer told me about moss-crop, "a little yellow flower that comes up in March, when there wasn't much grass of any sort and t'heather was as dead as matchsticks. After the flower dies down it becomes those white things on bent." He was referring to what the romantic call cotton grass and which Chris Cheetham or Kathleen Mattinson called a sedge. "A sheep likes it when it's yellow. It runs from one to another, snapping it off." Its nose is "fair breet" [bright] at moss-crop time. The moor sheep were horned, country-bred. "Then they got to breeding 'em, rather different, and called 'em Dales-bred." My favourite old farmer told about men who went off for the day to get new tups for their stock. Sometimes, a man who was on t'spree [sustained drinking session] got home without the tup he bought and had to go back looking for it.

Moss illness [calcium deficiency] was a terrible complaint. A lot of sheep were lost to it. By the time we lived at Austwick, the complaint was under control and "if thou can catch 'em thou can give 'em an injection – and in an hour they're on their feet again."

IONICUS

Epilogue

The neighbouring villages of Clapham and Austwick have featured strongly in my life. I worked in Clapham for forty years and lived – really lived – in Austwick for seven of them. One of Mrs Bee's daughters, whose memory of the places goes back further than mine, and who went to school at Clapham, mentioned skirmishes in the long-established warfare between the two.

"We at Austwick always felt we were superior to Clapham because we were free and didn't have a lord to lord it over us. Also their water was a funny colour. They could only retaliate by making up stories about cuckoos. Harry Scott, who edited the *Yorkshire Dalesman*, always led the anti-Austwick tease, of course, but Mrs Scott, presumably realising I was outnumbered, backed me up and thanked me when I offered to bring them some decent clean water from Austwick."

In the formative years, work at *The Dalesman* was done in the drawing room. "All the paper and copies were stored in the bedroom above until the ceiling began to cave in and Mr Scott feared that if he went up to shift it, his weight would bring the whole lot down. So the three of us little 'uns were sent up to crawl along and push it all towards the door so that the grown-ups could carry it downstairs."

Apart from keeping a pig in a sty, the Scotts had bantams in cages. Mrs Bee waged constant war against this. Their bantams should be free as were her hens. Harry Scott argued that if he did let them out, they always flew back to their cages, which showed they like them. Mrs Bee said this was because the poor things did not know anything better…

Going back to the two villages today is a deeply moving experience. Much has happened since we left for a home on t'other side of Buckhaw Brow. Time, the ever-rolling stream, has made a natural cull of most of those we knew and has brought into the villages people who the old-time Dalesfolk would have "wintered and summered and wintered again" before accepting them.

Every step I take evokes memories of the communities as they were half a century ago. I think of the Scotts sorting out *The Dalesman* mail at the breakfast table, amid the cups of tea, plates of toast and jars of home-made marmalade. I bring to mind Mrs Scott making herb beer in the cellar and apple dumplings with crusty suet pastry in her little pantry. In my happy remembrances, Caveman Brown is still the guide to Ingleborough Cave and uses the big key to play a tune on a row of stalactites.

The Dodgsons are at the village shop and Mr Brown presides over the post office. Grannie Cross, returning from a Women's Institute trip, opens her umbrella to release a host of cuttings she took in the gardens they visited – and then worries because there is little room in her overcrowded plot for new settlers. Mrs Vant walks down to the bus stop with a basket over one arm. In the basket is her pet duck.

(She broke the egg on to a hot water basket and reared the infant to maturity).

At Austwick, my mind switches to the unforgettable Mrs Bee. She took up cider production, sometimes with explosive consequences as a bottle or two shattered while being kept in her pantry. I also picture her in the kitchen, attending to the honey harvest, and the rich amber liquid that flowed when honey had been separated from the combs. Austwick reminds me of Courting Night for a middle-aged couple who were chaperoned by mother, complete with Tilly lamp in case the power failed.

In the Austwick of my day-dreams, Miss Geldard is presiding once again over Cappleside. When she moved to this imposing house, it was called The Nook but she preferred to use the name of the Geldard family mansion at Rathmell.

I recall showing old slides of the village, while Laura Lord and Renee Truelove help me by laughing at my jokes and Thomas Thistlethwaite (known to one and all as Tommy Apple) says, periodically: "Thou's wrong theer, Bill." (His home was demolished to make way for new development, known in his honour as Applegarth). I picture the church choir, with Messrs Truelove and Cheetham standing side by side and the former's wooden leg creaking as the choir process back down the aisle at the close of a service. When a new vicar and his wife began visiting Settle for their groceries because the prices were lower, George Truelove quit the church, declaring loudly: "And me shouting my bloody guts out in t'choir to get the vicarage order, well, they'll not see me in t'choir again." He was as good as his word.

I think of Cuckoo Town in its splendid natural setting, surrounded by floriferous meadows, with a crystal clear beck and three majestic limestone peaks to provide every local view with a splendid backdrop. From a meadow comes the rasping voice of a corncrake. There's a curlew aloft, gliding and uttering its tremulous song. Of course, there's a cuckoo calling from the hill, keeping well clear of the village where the men tried to wall in one of its ancestors.

Castleberg Books

by the same author

Birds of the Yorkshire Dales	£6.50
Ghost-hunting in the Yorkshire Dales	£5.99
Music of the Yorkshire Dales	£5.99
Sacred Places of the Lake District	£6.50
Beatrix Potter – Her Life in the Lake District	£6.20
The Lost Village of Mardale	£5.60
Garsdale – History of a Junction Station	£6.50
Mile by Mile on the Settle to Carlisle	£5.99
The Men Who Made the Settle to Carlisle	£5.99
Garsdale, Junction Station	£6.50
Life in the Lancashire Milltowns	£5.99
Nowt's Same	£6.50
You're Only Old Once	£4.99

Mini biographies:

Tot Lord and the Bone Caves	£4.50
Edith Carr – Life on Malham Moor	£4.50
Edward Elgar in the Yorkshire Dales	£4.99

All **Castleberg** titles are available at good bookshops
or, in case of difficulty, please write to:

North Yorkshire Marketing,
22 Azerley Grove, Harrogate,
North Yorkshire HG3 2SY

We will be pleased to send you a complete list of titles
and an order form

No postage is charged on **Castleberg** books